MISSION TRENDS TODAY

FOIM Series

FOIM V

MISSION TRENDS TODAY

HISTORICAL AND THEOLOGICAL PERSPECTIVES

Edited by: **Joseph Mattam
Sebastian Kim**

ST PAULS

Copyright 1997 Fellowship of Indian Missiologists (FOIM)

ISBN 81-7109-313-2

ST PAULS is an activity
of priests and brothers of the Society of St Paul
who proclaim the Gospel
through the media of Social Communication.

Printed by J. Njarakkatt at St Paul Press Training School,
Nagasandra, Bangalore and published by
ST PAULS, Bandra, Mumbai 400 050
1997

Contents

Contents

Introduction

Reflection on mission is a rather recent phenomenon in the churches. But today the need for regular reflection on mission to make it more and more suited to the people and their need is clear. In the past, missiology has been regarded as a matter of missionary methodology, namely, "how to do mission"; but discussions on mission in the latter half of the twentieth century have been focused on "what is mission". In other words, the search for a better understanding of the nature of mission has been the dominant concern. These reflections are very important because the definition of mission determines the methodology of mission rather than *vice versa*. The older understanding of mission has been very much challenged as Christians constantly face different contexts of poverty, injustice, other religions, and many other issues both inside and outside the church.

It is not possible to give one answer to the question "What is mission?", just as we now recognize that there is not one Christian theology or one universally accepted doctrine. Rather, there are many dimensions to the nature of mission, reflecting the diversity of its contexts. As our search for a definition of mission in our context shows, the nature of mission has been constantly changing over the years, reflecting our continuous quest to be part of *missio Dei,* which calls us to be faithful to Him and to His world.

In this volume, we have selected a few papers which attempt to reflect on some of the most important aspects of the nature of mission: social concern, missionary christology, ecumenical endeavour, popular religions, laity, missionary spirituality, worship, dialogue and church growth. We also have separate papers on the Catholic and Protestant trends in understanding of mission examined through major mission documents. The approach of the writers is mainly historical and theological; this enables the reader to have an overview of mission trends. These papers are of the 5th Annual Meeting of FOIM held at Pune from 16-19 August, 1996.

J. Saldanha offers a summary of the missiological thrust in the official documents of the Catholic Church. This survey reveals

7

that though missionary activity is as old as the Church itself, yet systematic reflection on this activity in the official documents of the Roman Catholic Church begins only in the 20th century. Many wise directives emanated from the Propaganda Congregation, but they were observed rather in the breach. The teaching of the bishops of Rome and of the Second Vatican General Council reflect the changing and wide-ranging needs and situations of the Church in mission in all countries of the world. At the present time, the reflections and recommendations of the Federation of Asian Bishops' Conference (FABC) witness to the effort of the Asian churches to fulfil their responsibility as local or particular churches.

F. Hrangkuma traces the Protestant mission trends in India. Unlike Catholics, the Protestant churches do not have authoritative and official documents; hence the documents studied here are products of Conferences and Consultations of interdenominational groups among Protestants. Following Duraisingh mission is seen as conquest for Christ, Christian presence, as bringing a new quality of life in India, a witnessing to the inner working of the spirit everywhere and finally as search for community in dialogue. He studies the Devlali letter of 1977, the WCC-CCA-NCCI Joint Consultation of 1991, the Statement of the International Conference on Mission 1994 and the Statement of the Mission-Evangelism Study Project 1996. These documents stress the need to start all missiological considerations on the one hand from the Bible, and on the other, from contemporary contexts. These are called "Missiology from above" and "Missiology from below". Both have their strengths and weaknesses, hence they need to dialogue.

J. Mattam studies the social concern in some of the official Catholic documents and among theologians. Among the official documents the study refers to the Roman documents, their background, influences which led to a new thrust in mission, and to the CBCI and FABC documents. From among the vast missiological literature, the study focuses on Samuel Rayan as a representative of this thrust among Catholic theologians. Searching out many of his unpublished works this paper makes available to people the rich and challenging insights of Rayan. He begins with a critique of the older understanding of mission which was other-worldly oriented, triumphalistic and dualistic. A new awareness has emerged due partly to the rise of Marxism, liberation theology and a better grasp of other religions. Rayan comments afresh on the mission command texts of the Bible. For a new concept of mission, he looks to the unity of the plan of God, a new concept of mission territory which sees the territory not primarily as geographical but something personal, having to do with structures, human behaviour and relations. He insists on mission commands like "be light, salt, leaven and fragrance". A lengthy section is devoted to development and evangelization, which emphasises mission as translating God's justice for the earth, as love made visible, as a spirituality of justice.

Mission demands a missionary christology, argues **J. Kavunkal**. The dilemma of a Hindu convert caught between loyalty to Christ and the healing of his dear ones who may get healed through some of the Hindu rituals is the dilemma the author feels about Christ and other religions. The paper looks at Jesus Christ in the context of religious pluralism. Beginning with his own faith experience, he attempts to open to the mystery wherever it is found. He approaches the mystery from the perspective of divine wisdom which is incarnated in Christ. The wisdom at work in creation is revealed in Jesus Christ. This reference to the wisdom helps us to understand the church's relation to other religions and the whole of creation. A christology based on Jesus as the divine wisdom incarnate can undergird the Christian approach to other religions in a positive way and promote inter-religious harmony without compromising Christian faith in the decisive and universal significance of Jesus Christ. The Mystery we call Jesus is universal and belongs to all religions. Since a historical person does not exhaust the divine wisdom, we can speak of the universal meaning of Jesus and the historical limits of Jesus. Other religions too participate in the divine wisdom. Jesus is to be seen as God's love in action — hence the ministry of Jesus is the key element in a missionary christology.

In Ecumenical Endeavour and Mission **S. and K. Kim** discuss the way in which mission and unity belong together. They note that the twentieth century movement for unity was initially for the sake of mission. But more recently in the Ecumenical Movement unity has become the aim of mission. They see a tendency in the gatherings of the World Council of Churches toward an identification of mission and unity on the theological basis of *missio Dei*, the cosmic Christ and the unbound nature of the Spirit. But a confusion of mission and unity has been consistently opposed by Evangelical Christians. The authors trace the development of this debate to conclude that a creative tension between mission and unity best expresses the complementarity of these closely related but distinct concepts.

J. Valiamangalam responds to the challenge of recent Catholic Church documents like *Evangelii Nuntiandi* which urge the local churches to "discover the people" and their culture and religion. These documents have highlighted the need to take popular religions seriously by the churches and those interested in mission. Popular religion is based on the experience of solidarity and compassion among the ordinary and poor people and is distinguished from that which is institutional and official. It is attractive to the masses; it is a cry of hope of the masses who desire to live in fraternity, justice and equality. The churches are challenged to enter into a deep and sympathetic study of popular religions. The mission of dialogue in India should be a dialogue more with the people's religion rather than with the institutionalized ones. Christian missionaries were pioneers in the empirical study of culture and popular religions; now too the churches are called by Christ through their evangelizing activity to get involved in the lives of ordinary people.

J. Patmury traces the meaning of laity from the Greek word *laikos* denoting 'of or from the people' which is intimately connected with the word *ekklesia*, meaning a called out people. He argues that in the early Christianity, the laity, both men and women, enjoyed positions of leadership and responsibility in the church, comparable to the clergy, especially since the organisation of the church was centred round the house churches. Before the end of the second century, there was a move away from house churches to dedicated churches; with this there arose a clergy and the church began to develop from now on more as a clerical society rather than as the people of God. Increasing clericalization, especially since Constantine, culminating in the excessive accumulation of power in the hands of the clergy in the Middle Ages would alienate the best lay intellects in the church, paving the way for the secularisation of the traditional Christian countries. There is however a better understanding of the role of the laity in modern times and laymen and laywomen are now beginning to take responsibility for the mission of the church in a more effective way.

M. Lobo raises certain fundamental questions: what do we mean by spirituality? How do we discover the stirring of the Spirit in the struggles and hopes of the people and in the processes of nature? Is it feasible to talk of a specific missionary spirituality in the Christian churches and what is its thrust? What is the dialectic between missionary spirituality and the context? Answering these questions Lobo maintains that the Spirit is manifest in the way one responds to the situation. Therefore the spirituality of those engaged in the church's mission — while being rooted in the gospel values — will have specific nuances marked by the Indian reality. This spirituality can open new pathways in the life and mission of the universal Church. As disciples of Jesus in India, missionaries have to discover the Jesus of faith and the vision of God's realm that moved him. This will give Indian missionary spirituality a much needed prophetic dynamism. Indian missionaries who live the Gospel from an experience of their context have important spiritual values to offer to the universal Church. Indian missionaries in pilgrimage with all people can affirm that ultimately God as Spirit is "Fullness from Fullness".

S. Prakash considers "Worship As Mission". Traditionally worship was considered as a function within the church and mission as a duty to the outside; the author shows that the two belong together inseparably to the very nature of the church and that worship itself is mission. Both mission and worship aim at restoring wholeness and fuller life to every creature. Worship has a sense of gathering and sending, it is centripetal and centrifugal. Mission is celebration in worship. Worship in general, and more particularly baptism and the eucharist, are intrinsically related to

11

the mission, just as Jesus' baptism was the beginning of his mission. The author shows that the various aspects of worship like prayer, thanksgiving, intercession, confession of faith and of sin, reading and sermon have a mission dimension. The author considers that worship plays an important role in providing the church with the content and context for its mission in the world.

J. Thomas in "Dialogue As evangelizing Mission" returns to the II Vatican Council's invitation to "consider dialogue as part of the church's evangelizing mission in a multi-religious context. The focus of this paper is on dialogue of life and action leading all religious institutes and movements to meet and enter into "kingdom ministries" to help build up a new humanity. The author's own early experience of lived dialogue when he lived, prayed, studied and worked together with Hindus and Muslims is in sharp contrast to the official demands for dialogue from a position of superiority and with hidden agendas. He emphasizes the presence of the Spirit of God in every true dialogue. The Popes while calling for dialogue, insist on "the church as the ordinary means of salvation" and the need for missionary activity to bring in all into the church, betray the "church's fundamentalist attitude" of lack of true respect for other religions. In spite of the ambiguities, dialogue as an attitude is indispensable. The author invites all believers to move to *communicatio in sacris*, to enter into the religious experience of others. In the context of growing communalism, true dialogue may be the only means to preserve religions from becoming mere instruments in the hands of politicians. Only if all religions are truly committed to the service of humanity will dialogue be real.

Finally, **J. Chacko** looks at "Mission as Church Growth". The Church Growth Movement based on the seminal works of Bishop W. Picket and Dr D. McGavran emphasizes the need for people movement rather than individual accessions. This movement prohibits crossing of cultural barriers and sets its goal as numerical growth with concentration on those areas that show growing receptivity to Christianity. While emphasizing numerical growth, this movement may not be accused of "numerolatry", for the "present institutional success is on the basis of the future of God's kingdom". This movement has been a real challenge to missionary enterprise by insisting on group conversions. However it has its own problems and weaknesses: a shallow hermeneutic, absence of a solid theological foundation and a truncated concept of mission, playing down the societal and justice dimension of the Gospel. By insisting on the "Homogeneous Unit Principle", it neglects the wider principle of Christian brotherhood/sisterhood. This movement still needs to take a holistic approach to mission.

This volume touches upon various important dimensions of mission today. We hope these stimulating studies will help the readers to deepen their love for the mission entrusted to the Church by her Lord and recommit themselves to carry on proclaiming the good news of God's salvation in Christ. This will provide valuable resource material and stimulation for all students and teachers of missiology.

The opinions expressed are of the authors themselves and not of the group. Our grateful thanks are due to all those who have helped in the typing, proof-reading and publishing of this work.

Joseph Mattam   *Sebastian Kim*

CHAPTER 1

Mission Trends
in the Official Documents
of the Roman Catholic Church

Julian Saldanha*

I. Introduction

The missionary imperative has always been taken for granted since the origin of the Church, so that missionary activity is as old as the Church itself. However, it is only in the 20th century that it began to be a subject of systematic reflection, study and research. The first Catholic Chair of Missiology was founded in Munster in 1911; there the same year was published the first technical periodical on the subject. W. Buhlmann could refer to missiology as "a late child of theology" (1963:353-359). This situation is reflected in the official documents of the Roman Catholic Church. Vatican II (1965) was the first General Council of the Church to treat of missionary activity. The First Vatican General Council (1870) intended to consider a (rather juridical) draft text on the missions, but never came to it. The bishops of Rome very gradually began to play an increasingly active role in the direction of the Church's missionary activity. However, the first Roman bishop to deal at length with various aspects of "the propagation of the faith

---

* Julian Saldanha holds a doctorate in missiology. Formerly Provincial Superior of the Bombay Province of the Society of Jesus, he is the author of numerous missiological articles and books. He presently lectures at Goregaon Seminary and is the President of the Fellowship of Indian Missiologists.

throughout the world" was Benedict XV, in his Encyclical letter, *Maximum Illud* (1919). Prior to this, we have a few stray references to certain aspects of missionary activity in the decrees of some Councils and the writings of some Roman bishops.

In this chapter I limit myself to the teaching and directives of General Councils, of the bishops of Rome and of the Congregation for the Propagation of the Faith ("Propaganda" for short). I conclude with a section on the Federation of Asian Bishops' Conferences.

II. Up to the Founding of "Propaganda" (-1622)

The First General Council of Nicaea (325) recommended a catechesis of adequate duration for new converts to the faith. They must not be promoted to the episcopate or presbyterate without a long probation after baptism (Neuner & Dupuis 1973n.1101). In a famous instruction for the Anglo-Saxon mission in the year 601, Gregory 'the Great', bishop of Rome, counselled the consecration of temples, sacrifices and sacred meals to the honour of the true God: "they will sacrifice and eat the animals not any more as an offering to the devil, but for the glory of God". His instructions also influenced the methods of the Anglo-Saxon missionaries on the Continent. He had at first instructed Augustine, apostle of England, to extirpate everything non-Christian. But he found that this did not achieve the goal; besides, did not God instruct the Israelites to use the Egyptian sacrifices for his own cult (Saldanha 1988:48)? The attitude towards believers of other religions became gradually very narrow. The Fourth Lateran General Council (1215) legalized discrimination against Jews, by decreeing that they must be distinguished by their dress from Christians and be excluded from holding public office. The General Council of Vienna (1311-12) meeting during the prolonged crusade for the liberation of the Holy Land from the Saracens, decreed that the cult rendered to Mohammed by the Saracens must be forbidden in lands under Catholic rulers. The 17th General Council meeting in Basel in 1434, decreed that Jews are to be forced under pain of various penalties to attend sermons on the Christian faith, which might lead to their conversion. The same Council meeting in Florence in 1442 "firmly" taught that "no one remaining outside the Catholic Church, not only pagans, but also Jews, heretics or schismatics, can become partakers of eternal life ..." (Neuner n. 290-291, 810). In the 16th century most of the above stipulations of these Councils were extended also to Hindus in Goa. The councils both of Vienna and Basel insisted on the preachers of the Gospel being well versed in the languages needed for the evangelisation of the Muslims.

In keeping with the general approach of the times, one aimed at the conversion of the rulers, expecting that their subjects would follow suit. Thus Pope Innocent IV addressed two letters to the Emperor of the Mongols in March 1245. He briefly expounded the Christian faith and told him to desist from attacking Christian countries and to "acknowledge Jesus Christ the very Son of God and worship his glorious name by practising the Christian religion". He received a retort from Guyuk Khan, grandson of Chingis Khan. Guyuk Khan found the Pope's exhortation "impudent": "You men of the West believe that you alone are Christians and despise others." Far from becoming a "trembling Nestorian Christian", he exhorted the Pope "at the head of all the Princes, to come at once to serve and wait upon us!" (Dawson :73-86). Likewise Pope Gregory XIII addressed a letter to the Emperor Akbar on 18 February 1582, urging him to embrace the Christian faith (Correia-Afonso :119-120). It is well known that during the colonial mission period, Christianity spread in close conjunction with the commercial, political and military expansion of European powers. The spirit of the times is expressed in a letter (1567) of Pope Pius V to the Portuguese Viceroy of India and his Council: "As more and more gentiles accept the Christian faith, so the king's glorious name will become more glorious, his rule in these parts will be more firmly established, he will acquire greater power to subjugate uncultured nations with divine assistance and join them to the Portuguese empire" (Saldanha 1988:119).

III. The Congregation
for the Propagation of the Faith

A new spirit and impulse for missionary activity came with

17

the founding of the "Congregation for the Propagation of the Faith" by Pope Gregory XV in 1622. After Vatican II, it was renamed "Congregation for the Evangelisation of Peoples". This event marked the beginning of a greater centralization of missionary activity and independence from State control. Propaganda also introduced many sound principles in missionary method which, unfortunately, were often half-heartedly, if at all, implemented by the authorities in the missions. Propaganda warned missionaries against exaggerated European nationalism and the zeal to spread European culture in the missions; they must learn the local languages well and foster all wholesome local customs; they are not to seek commercial gain; in particular, they must train a local clergy as soon as possible. (In 1627 Pope Urban VIII founded a college in Rome for the training of candidates from the younger churches to the priesthood).

These themes are best illustrated in the celebrated Instruction which Propaganda gave the first bishops, Vicars Apostolic of Tonkin and Cochinchina in 1659; these areas were then outside colonial domains. The bishops were to keep "far away from political affairs and businesses of State". They must train a local clergy and episcopate and must not persuade those people to change their rites, customs and ways, "provided they are not very manifestly contrary to religion and morals. For, what is more absurd than to introduce France, Spain or Italy, or any other part of Europe into China? It is not these things, but the faith that you must bring in ...". Nevertheless, the scope for practising this was rather limited, as may be gauged from the fact that in 1755 Propaganda sternly warned a certain missionary not to use any Chinese in the Mass. And in the Malabar rites controversy, Pope Benedict XIV severely forbade the omission, in baptism, of the use of saliva, a practice abhorrent to Indians. In 1744 he ordered the missionaries "in virtue of holy obedience" to extirpate their neophytes' horror of the rite. (Saldanha 1988:68, 122-3). It must be added, that Propaganda made a reluctant compromise with caste discrimination in the Church (Saldanha 1996).

18

IV. Encyclicals Prior to Vatican II (1919-1959)

1. Goal of Mission

We must now turn to the Encyclical Letters on missionary activity, written by the bishops of Rome in modern times. (They are listed at the end of this chapter.) These dealt with diverse facets of missionary activity and provided much encouragement and guidance. The mission is to aim at the conversion of people to the Christian faith, with a view to the "expansion" or "extension" of the Church. In continuity with his recent predecessors, Pius XII described the "final goal" of the missions as "the establishment of the Church in new territories". John XXIII quoted approvingly the words of Pius XII: "The ultimate aim of all missionary activity — and this must never be lost sight of — is to plant the Church firmly among the peoples of other lands and to give them their own hierarchy, chosen from among their own people."

It was this concern that moved Pius XII to issue a special appeal in 1957 (*Fidei Donum*) on behalf of Africa, where Islam was then spreading: "Twenty more priests in a particular region would make it possible to plant the cross there today, while tomorrow this same land, tilled by other workers than those of the Lord, will probably have become impervious to the true Faith."

2. Role of Local Clergy and Laity

Benedict XV lamented: "Notwithstanding the Roman Pontiff's insistence... it is sad to think that there are nations... who have reached such a degree of civilisation as to possess men distinguished in every department of secular knowledge; who for many centuries have come under the salutary influence of the Gospel and the Church, and have yet been able to yield neither bishops to rule them, nor priests to direct them." Pius XI explained that the indigenous priest is in touch with his people and knows their language well. He knows "better than anyone else the best methods to follow" and can gain access where a foreign priest could never enter. With prophetic vision he urged, that a great safeguard for local churches, from which foreign missionaries have been expelled by a change of government, would be "a network

19

of native priests throughout the whole country". He felt constrained to counter the prejudice, that the local people are "of an inferior race and of obtuse intelligence". Indigenous clergy must not be "used only for the most humble offices of the ministry... Let there not be any discrimination, therefore, between European and native missionaries". He followed this up by ordaining six Chinese bishops in Rome in 1926.

At the same time, the laity were exhorted to collaborate with the clergy in their apostolate through various forms of "Catholic Action". They were encouraged to "join other organisations whose purpose is to reform social and political life according to the principles and teaching of the Gospel". Pius XII traced the sterling contribution made by the laity to the Church's mission since New Testament times (Popes :56-59). Singled out for special mention are the Catechists, "the missionaries' right-hand men" (John XXIII).

3. Human Promotion

While opening institutions for the poor, Pius XI counselled missionaries "not to neglect the nobles of the region and their children... (For) history and experience teach us that when once the leaders of the people have been converted to Christianity, the ordinary people follow closely in their footsteps". Pius XII noted that "the Catholic Church has not only advanced its spiritual kingdom, but has also led nations to increased social prosperity". He condemned "the various forms of Marxist socialism", but supported "social reforms demanded by justice and charity". The Popes and Propaganda repeatedly stressed the importance of mission schools as a means of: a) forming Christian youth and preserving their faith; b) training leaders of Catholic Action; c) disposing non-Christian youth to the Christian faith; some of these might be tomorrow's leaders; d) gaining influence and good will among all classes of society; e) refuting errors, e.g. Communism. They viewed the works of charity in the missions as: a) a sign of the Kingdom of God; they represent the activity of Christ who went about doing good; b) they prepare the way for conversion; they lead non-Christians to reflect on and praise Christianity;

c) missionaries should remember Christ's loving kindness towards children.

Benedict XV was aware that some missionaries were bent upon extending the power and glory of their own country. This, he said, was also reflected in recently published mission accounts, which "make very painful reading for us". He denounced this as "a plague most deadly to their apostolate", and warned: "You are not to enrol citizens into any country of this world, but that of the next."

4. Respect for Local Cultures

Pius XII stated that the Gospel, on being introduced into new lands, should not "destroy or extinguish whatever its people possess that is naturally good, just or beautiful... Whatever there is in the native customs that is not inseparably bound up with superstition and error will always receive kindly consideration and, when possible, will be preserved intact". And John XXIII visualised local priests "following in the footsteps of that most celebrated missionary Matteo Ricci". However, in practice, there was little scope to implement these directives. Pius XII saw it as part of the Church's role to "call people to a higher culture". Nevertheless, the tone was less condescending than that of Benedict XV, who saw "priests of civilised nations" going "to announce Christ to uncivilised nations". And Pius XI referred to "the heathens, particularly those who are still savages and barbarians".

The missionary should have a thorough knowledge of the language of the people to whom he is sent, so as to enjoy "a fluent and elegant command" over it (Benedict XV; this point would be reiterated by Vatican II, *Ad Gentes* 26). Pius XI wanted the bishops "to consider as one of the principal duties of your office the founding of native religious Congregations of both men and women... such as may answer better the genius and character of the natives, and be more in keeping with the needs and spirit of the country".

5. Other Religions

The attitude towards other religions and their followers is at best condescending and at worst negative. Benedict XV urged missionaries to have "compassion for the sad fate of this multitude of souls... sitting in the shadows of death, and to open the gate of heaven to those who rush to their destruction". In fostering "missions among infidels", he spoke of "the Gentile races which, in ignorance of God, are enslaved to blind and unbridled instincts, and live under the awful servitude of the evil one... (under) Satan's proud dominion". The greatest charity one can show one's neighbours, said Pius XI, was to "have them withdrawn from the darkness of superstition and instructed in the true faith of Christ". Thus one would "smooth the way to salvation for heathen nations".

6. Other Directives and Measures

The most important quality of the apostolic labourer is sanctity of life. Still, as part of their training, future missionaries "should be sufficiently instructed in the sciences of medicine, agriculture, ethnography, history, geography, and so on", since these will be most useful to them in the mission lands. All should offer the support of their prayer, which is "the very nourishment of the missions". Specially commended are the services of women, particularly Sisters. Recommended is the use of the print media to spread the truth and to expose fallacies and prejudices against the Christian faith; the *Fides* news service was started for the same purpose in Rome. The Roman bishops founded the "Missionary Union of the Clergy" and of the "Holy Childhood" to pray for the missions and to spread knowledge about them; also the organisation of St Peter the Apostle, to distribute subsidies to seminaries in mission countries. University chairs of missiology were founded in Rome and elsewhere.

One is impressed by the detailed treatment of the multifarious dimensions of missionary activity, by the bishops of Rome. Today it is easier to recognise some shortcomings in their mission theology. Nevertheless, it may be said that they paved the way for the "Decree on the Church's Missionary Activity" (*Ad Gentes*) by Vatican II.

V. The Second Vatican General Council (1962-65)

The core text on mission, which would be developed in other documents of Vatican II, especially in *Ad Gentes*, is contained in the "Constitution on the Church" (*Lumen Gentium* 13-17). However, I shall limit myself chiefly to *Ad Gentes*. This document traces the origin of the mission to the divine Trinitarian life, which explains why "the pilgrim Church is missionary by her very nature" (n.2), and "the whole Church is missionary" (n.35). Hence also the urgency of missionary activity: "though God in ways known to himself can lead those inculpably ignorant of the gospel to that faith without which it is impossible to please him (Heb 11:6), yet a necessity lies upon the Church (cf. 1 Cor 9:16)... to preach the gospel" (n.7). Chapter 1 mentions several motives of missionary activity, including its eschatological finality. The specific purpose of missionary activity is "the planting of the Church among those peoples and groups where she has not yet taken root... the chief means of this implantation is the preaching of the gospel of Jesus Christ" (n.6).

The Decree has a pastoral and ecumenical orientation and is grounded in Scripture. Besides collaborating in social, cultural and religious projects, Christians should "make before the nations a common profession of faith in God and in Jesus Christ" (n.15). It was explained to the Council Fathers, that "adaptation" was on purpose not given separate treatment, precisely because it is of such great importance and has so many diverse aspects: it needed rather to compenetrate the document and emerge throughout it. In this the document has succeeded. The young churches, receiving the word of God as a seed, are to grow according to the model of the incarnation, drawing nourishing elements from their culture, "in a wonderful exchange" (n.22). Numbers 10-12 describe mission in terms of social insertion. An accent is placed on dialogue with non-Christians, formation of the Christian community and the apostolate of the laity, diversity in unity of the particular churches. Chapter IV develops a very high ideal of missionary spirituality and formation. As regards the approach to other religions, *Ad Gentes* had before it the Council's "Declaration on the Relationship of the Church to Non-Christian Religions" (n.2), which exhorted Catholics "...in witness of Christian faith and life, to acknowledge, preserve and promote the spiritual and moral goods found among these people, as well as the values in their society and culture".

The missionary bishops at the Council keenly felt the burden of history, which they wished to shake off. Especially since the last century, the missions have been reproached with colonialism, neo-colonialism, imperialism, the mix-up of mission and politics, Western arrogance and racial pride (Schütte 1967:9-20). Hence the mission is described in terms of service and respect for cultures and religions; the spiritual perspectives are highlighted. After some debate, the Council reaffirmed the role of the Propaganda Congregation, to "direct and coordinate missionary work" throughout the world. It is to be "both an administrative instrument and an agency of dynamic direction" (n.29). The former "mission churches" are now referred to as "young churches" and a special Chapter III is devoted to them. They are thus placed on an equal level with all the other churches and are as much subjects of missionary activity as the others. Many of the young churches are sending an ever increasing number of missionaries to other countries. Indian missionaries serving abroad (over 2000) greatly outnumber the foreign missionaries serving in India (Saldanha 1990).

Ad Gentes marked an important moment in the missionary consciousness of the Roman Catholic Church. It was the first time that the young churches were represented by their own bishops in such large numbers at a General Council. As Karl Rahner stated, it was at Vatican II that for the first time "the Church began *in fact* to actualize itself precisely as a world Church". However, *Ad Gentes* was being overtaken by new developments which were already underway in missionary thinking and practice, and which would necessitate a Synod of bishops in Rome in 1974. Drawing on the rich material presented by this Synod, Pope Paul VI issued an encyclical letter, "Evangelii Nuntiandi" (EN), through which he desired to "invigorate" his brethren "in these uncertain and troubled times". This encyclical remains largely unsurpassed up to the present day (Saldanha 1979).

VI. Evangelii Nuntiandi (1975)

I wish to draw attention to certain issues which are treated here, but did not figure in *Ad Gentes*.

1. Terms

The terms "missionary", in noun or adjectival form, and "missions" are always used in the context of work among non-Christians. *Ad Gentes* also used these terms in the same sense. Furthermore, the Council distinguished missionary activity "from pastoral activity exercised among the faithful, as well as from undertakings aimed at restoring unity among Christians" (AG 6). Until the post-Conciliar time, the word "evangelisation" was little used in the Catholic Church; Vatican II uses it only about 31 times. The Council speaks rather of "missionary activity". But in EN the expression "evangelisation" (or "evangelise") is employed frequently throughout. In the outlook of EN, there is only one mission of the Church in the world and it is traced back to the mission of Jesus, aimed at the Kingdom of God. This single mission is accomplished in a variety of spheres (spiritual, social, cultural etc.), and not only among atheists and followers of other religions but also Catholics and other Christians. All that the Church does in fulfilling this mission is called "evangelisation".

To sum up, EN does not reject the terms "missions" and "missionary" as used by AG. But these concepts are situated more clearly and forcefully within the single comprehensive mission of the Church, which is entitled "evangelisation". Although the phrase "planting the Church" occurs nowhere in EN, the birth and growth of indigenous churches is certainly envisaged: however, not as an end in themselves but as "sign and instrument of the Kingdom of God".

2. The Church in Constant Need of Being Evangelised

The Church evangelises through the witness of her life and preaching (nn.21-22), through deeds and words having an inner unity: the deeds confirm and illustrate the words, while the words explain the deeds. To this end the Church has to practise what she preaches. "The Church begins her task by evangelizing herself...

25

by constant conversion and renewal, in order to evangelise the world with credibility" (nn.15, 52, 54, 58).

In this context must be placed the quality of *authenticity* which the Pope stresses: "Modern man listens more willingly to witnesses than to teachers, and if he does listen to teachers, it is because they are witnesses" (nn.41; 21, 76). They must witness not only to union with the "Absolute" Who is God, but also to solidarity with people. They must be at the same time more ardent in contemplation and adoration and more zealous in charitable and liberating action.

3. Popular Piety (n. 48)

It offers much scope for evangelisation. It would include such expressions of the search for God and for faith as pilgrimages, religious festivals, novenas and other devotions, especially those connected with Lent and Holy Week. These forms of piety were for long considered less pure and were sometimes despised, but modern investigation results in a constructive evaluation of them. Popular piety is open to the dangers of superstition and mere external religion. "But if it is well oriented... it is rich in values". It manifests a thirst for God as loving, provident Father and it fosters generosity, patience, detachment, even heroic sacrifice. It is truly "the religion of the people". This topic was discussed in the Synod of 1974, especially by the delegates from Latin America.

4. Small Communities or "Communautés de Base" (n. 58)

These refer to small groupings of Christians linked by age, culture or social situation, in villages or cities. Such "grass-roots" communities have sprung up throughout the Church and satisfy the need to live the Church's life more intensely. Certain guidelines are proposed so that they may offer hope to the Church and be "seedbeds of evangelisation". They must "unite themselves to the Church and cause the Church to grow".

5. Liberation

This term occurs for the first time in a papal document in *Octogesima Adveniens* (1971), which borrowed it from the

Medellin Conference of 1968. The word is used frequently in Chapter III of EN. Already Vatican II (GS 26) saw a sign of the times in the world-wide desire for a more humane social order built on justice, animated by love and requiring widespread changes in attitudes and in society.

In EN (Chpt III) the Pope insists that the Church has "the duty" to further liberation from famine, chronic diseases, illiteracy, indigence, economic neo-colonialism: "this is not foreign to evangelisation". The redemption of creation and of people requires the restoration of justice in the very concrete situations of life. Furthermore, how can one preach the new commandment without promoting, in justice and peace, the authentic development of people? The Church associates herself with all who labour and suffer for liberation; she "does not accept a restriction of her mission only to the religious field". Therefore, "she is trying more and more to encourage large numbers of Christians to devote themselves to liberating others". This firm and unambiguous commitment to liberation corresponded with the desire of the Synod and particularly of bishops from the 'Third World'. What the Pope is chiefly concerned about is that the Christian struggle for liberation be inserted into the universal plan of that salvation which the Church proclaims.

6. Evangelisation of Cultures (nn. 18-20)

This is described as "affecting and as it were upsetting, through the power of the Gospel, humankind's criteria of judgement, determining values, points of interest, lines of thought, sources of inspiration and models of life, which are in contrast with the Word of God and the plan of salvation". This avoids a superficial adaptation of the Gospel message among a particular people. The Pope boldly invites the particular churches to "translate the treasure of faith into the legitimate variety of expressions of the profession of faith, of prayer and worship, of Christian life and conduct..." (n. 64).

EN, like AG earlier and RM later, maintains the importance of proclaiming the mystery of Christ to all people with confidence and constancy, "wherever God opens a door of speech"

(AG 13). At the same time one notices a growing concern that the redemption of Christ be made ever more effective and visible in human relationships and in the structures of society. Beyond verbal proclamation, the gospel is meant to be a force for the transformation of society.

7. Note on the Religions

In keeping with Vatican II, Paul VI acknowledges the 'seeds of the Word' in other religions, which can constitute a true 'preparation for the gospel' (AG 11; LG 16). Unfortunately, he does not develop this patristic line of thought which illumines the *divine* element in the religions of the world. He prefers to consider them as a *human effort* of searching for God. Hence they are called "natural religions" (n. 53). Not less unhappy is the distinction of Christianity as the "ordinary" way of salvation from the "extraordinary ways" by which God can save non-Christians (n. 80). EN says nothing about inter-religious dialogue (see further discussion of this point in Saldanha 1979:37-38). But in 1984 the Vatican Secretariat for inter-religious dialogue issued a document which stated that, "A person discovers that he does not possess the truth in a perfect and total way, but can walk together with others towards that goal... Dialogue is thus the norm and necessary manner of every form of Christian mission" including direct proclamation.[1]

VII. Redemptoris Missio (RM 1990)

This Encyclical was published by Pope John Paul II, on the occasion of the 25th anniversary of *Ad Gentes*. It focuses sharply on "missionary activity" rather than on the broader concept of "evangelisation" as found in EN. It repeats the warning in EN, against reducing the human person to his/her horizontal dimension. Important elements of a *theology/spirituality of development* are spelled out in numbers 58-60. The Church serves the Kingdom, among other ways, "by her intercession, since the Kingdom by its very nature is God's gift and work" (n. 20). In Chapter 2 the

---

[1] *L'Osservatore Romano*, 25/6/1984

Pope makes an admirable effort to clarify the relationship between Church-Christ-Kingdom. The Encyclical contains some welcome elements, which are not found in EN and which complete it.

1. Something New

Among the signs that God is preparing "a great springtime in Christianity" is the universal attraction for "*Gospel values*" or "*values of the Kingdom*". These phrases were current in missiological circles for a number of years, under the influence of liberation theology. They appear here for the first time in a missionary encyclical. The Church is described as "the sign and promoter of Gospel values". Some of these are listed in several parts of the encyclical: peace, justice, freedom, brotherhood, concern for the needy, respect for the human person and for human rights, the dignity and role of women.

The section on *Inter-Religious Dialogue* makes up for the glaring omission of the same in EN. RM paves the way for a more positive appreciation of other religions than is found in EN, by acknowledging in them "signs of Christ's presence and of the working of the Spirit". The Pope also admits that dialogue can lead to mutual enrichment and to "mutual advancement on the road of religious inquiry and experience". In other words, missionary activity is not meant to be a one-way project.

In the same spirit, the Pope affirms that through *inculturation* "the universal Church herself is enriched" in various areas of her life, including liturgy and theology. "Inculturation must involve the whole people of God, and not just a few experts". The first time this term was used in an official Church document was in the "Message to the People of God" of the bishops' Synod 1977.

Especially to be welcomed is the recognition of the *problems connected with conversion*. They display a special sensitivity to the peculiar situation prevailing in India. Today, as in the past, many people do not accept the Gospel revelation or enter the Church, because "the social and cultural conditions in which they live do not permit this, and frequently they have been brought up in other religious traditions... in some places sociological con-

29

siderations associated with baptism obscure its genuine meaning as an act of faith... many profess an interior commitment to Christ and his message yet do not wish to be committed sacramentally, since, owing to prejudice or because of the failings of Christians, they find it difficult to grasp the true nature of the Church as a mystery of faith and love".

The Pope's comments on the *importance of evangelisation in the 'megalopolises'* or big cities are stimulating and challenging.[2] It is here that "new customs and styles of living arise together with new forms of culture and communication, which then influence the wider population". The "option for the neediest" should not blind us to the fact that "individuals or small groups cannot be evangelised if we neglect the centres where a new humanity, so to speak, is emerging, and where new models of development are taking shape. The future of the younger nations is being shaped in the cities".

Among the Religious Institutes, the Pope singles out *Missionary Institutes of Sisters* for a special word of appreciation. By their example and activity, especially on behalf of the very poor, they are "an indispensable evangelical sign among those peoples and cultures where women still have far to go on the way towards human promotion and liberation".

2. Areas Requiring Greater Clarity

a) Goal of mission: On the one hand it is stated that "the Church is effectively and concretely at the service of the Kingdom", of which she is "the seed, sign and instrument". On the other hand, it is asserted that "the proclamation of the word of God has Christian conversion as its aim... This must be our motto: All the churches united for the conversion of the whole world". And: "The mission *Ad Gentes* has this objective: to found Christian communities...". All these elements have their place in missionary activity. However, it is important to be clear about their mutual

---

[2] It is estimated that by the year 2000, over half the world's population will be living in urban zones and about half the cities counting a *minimum* population of 5 million will be in Asia.

relationship in the context of the goal of mission. This has practical and pastoral consequences for the conduct of missionary activity.

b) **Christ and gospel values:** It would be helpful to spell out the relationship between our faith in and proclamation of Christ on the one hand, and our promotion of Gospel values on the other hand.

c) **Fullness of revelation:** The Pope speaks of the Church as having "the fullness of Revelation" and "the fullness of the truth". Such notions make dialogue difficult and need to be nuanced, especially since Vatican II states that the Church is still moving towards the fullness of divine truth ("Dogmatic Constitution on Divine Revelation", n. 8). Unfortunate also is the description of the Church as "the ordinary means of salvation". Such terminology lays itself open to the same critique which was made of the distinction drawn in EN between the "ordinary" way of salvation and the "extraordinary ways" by which God can save non-Christians.

VIII. The Federation of Asian Bishops' Conferences (FABC)

I would like to conclude this brief survey of mission trends in the Roman Catholic Church, with a reference to the efforts made by the Asian bishops after Vatican II to contextualize their mission in Asia. The FABC was formed just over two decades ago and held its first Plenary Assembly in 1974 on the theme of "Evangelisation in Modern Day Asia". Since then, much rich material for reflection and action has emanated from the Federation. This is available in Rosales 1992:, to which I refer in this section.

1. The Context

Nearly two-thirds of humanity live in this "vast and varied, restless and swiftly-changing" continent; 60 % are below 25 years of age. Here was the cradle of the most ancient cultures and world religions. Here too the wide gap between the poor and the affluent is often fuelled by an economy which caters to the demands of the market, rather than to the basic needs of the majority. Asia is in the throes of a deep cultural crisis, as it struggles to come to terms with modernity. No wonder, religious fundamentalism has been on the upswing and fully exploited by politicians. On the other hand, if we exclude the Philippines, Catholics account for less than 1% of Asia's population. What can be the mission of the Asian churches in this context?

2. Mission in Asia

A key element in the FABC response has been the call to a wide-ranging dialogue: "a church in continuous, humble and loving dialogue with the living traditions, the cultures, the religions — in brief, with all the life-realities of the people in whose midst it has sunk its roots deeply and whose history and life it gladly makes its own" (Rosales & Arevalo 1992:14). Working for and *with* the poor is part of the 'dialogue of life' with the poor. This is carried out in the awareness that the poor are rich in "cultural traditions, human values and religious insights"; the values include interiority, detachment, compassion and peace. "We therefore turn not only to our Christian resources, but also to those of other faiths, so that we might achieve mutual enrichment" (*ibid.* 230, 314, 321). The bishops stress the complementarity ('yinyang') which exists between peoples, cultures, faiths, ideologies, world-visions, etc., as something very characteristic of Asian traditions (*ibid.* 322).

Thus, "Mission will mean a dialogue with Asia's poor, with its local cultures, and with other religious traditions". This mission includes: "being with the people, responding to their needs, with sensitiveness to the presence of God in cultures and other religious traditions, and witnessing to the values of God's Kingdom through presence, solidarity, sharing and word". Christ is to be proclaimed above all by living like him and doing his deeds by the power of his grace (*ibid.* 280, 282). The process of inculturation grows out of this insertion: "A Church that stands with sisters and brothers of other faiths in confronting issues of life and death will necessarily be transformed in the process. In other words, it will become inculturated — at a level which includes but goes deeper than changes in ritual and symbol" (*ibid.* 333).

3. Building a Local Church

To carry out the mission described above requires "a truly local church... indigenous and inculturated... It seeks to share in whatever truly belongs to that people: its meanings and its values, its aspirations, its thoughts and its language, its songs and its artistry". For this reason, the First Plenary Assembly of the FABC (1974) stated: "The primary focus of our task of evangelisation then, at this time in our history, is the building up of a truly local church" (FABC:14).

The bishops candidly admitted their shortcomings in fulfilling this task: "Dialogue, sharing, co-responsibility are words that we use regularly, but now we clearly see that the vast majority of our laity do not share in dialogue with their clergy; nor do they share the responsibility for the work of the Church with their clergy in a partnership of brotherhood". Laity, bishops, priests and religious: all "need to update our vision of the Church and learn new methods and skills..." (FABC:235-236). In building the local church, one should keep in mind that, "The formation of Basic Christian Communities, which are self-reliant, should lead to the formation of Basic Human Communities. In this way, the Church of Asia can truly become servant of all" (FABC:254). Among the ministries which may be instituted for lay people are those of healing, of inter-religious dialogue and of community building (FABC:79-80). The Fourth Plenary Assembly (1986) noted that the image and likeness of God in Asian women "has been degraded and trampled underfoot and she is dominated in various ways". In this respect, the laity are reminded of their responsibility "to change attitudes, policies, practices and legislation that lead to the discrimination against and repression of women" (FABC 1986: 183).

IX. Conclusion

The regular exposure programmes for the bishops, organised by various offices of the FABC, influenced the bishop's perception of the Asian reality. There is no doubt that the Asian realities and outlook are reflected in the documents of the FABC.

33

Only in this way can the Asian churches make an original contribution to the other churches. The present survey of mission trends shows that the missionary consciousness has always been alive in the Church, but that new situations and challenges have led this pilgrim Church along new paths of mission. Obviously we will not reach the end of the road until Christ comes again!

References

Buhlmann, W. (1963) "Fifty years of Missiology" in *African Ecclesiastical Review*.

Correia-Afonso, J. (1980) *Letters from the Mughal Court*, Gujarat Sahitya Prakash: Anand

Dawson, C. (1955) *The Mongol Mission*, London: Sheed & Ward.

Neuner and Dupuis (ed.) (1973) *The Christian Faith*, Bangalore: TPI.

The Popes and the Missions: Sword of the Spirit, London, n.d.

Rosales & Arevalo (ed.) (1992) *For All the Peoples of Asia*, New York: Orbis Books.

Saldanha, J. (1979) "A Fresh Impulse for Evangelization in Our Times" in *Indian Missiological Review*, No.1. pp.23-43.

Saldanha, J. (1985) "The Teaching of Pope John Paul II on Evangelization", *Indian Missiological Review*, No.4, pp.358-369.

Saldanha, J. (1988) *Patterns of Evangelisation in Mission History*, Bombay: St Paul Publications.

Saldanha, J. (1990) "The Third Church is At Hand!", in *Vidyajyoti*, No.6, pp.295-299.

Saldanha, J. (1996) "Some Documents on Caste in the Church" in *Indian Missiological Review*, No.3, pp.54-58.

Schütte, J. (1967) *Mission Nach dem Konzil*, Mainz: Matthias-Grunewald Verlag.

Encyclical Letters on Missionary Activity

Benedict XV (1919) *Maximum Illud"* in *The Popes and the Missions.*

Pius XI (1926) *Rerum Ecclesiae* in *The Popes and the Missions.*

Pius XII (1951) *Evangelii Praecones* in *The Popes and the Missions.*

Pius XII (1957) *Fidei Donum* in *The Popes and the Missions.*

John XXIII (1960) *Princeps Pastorum*, London: Catholic Truth Society.

Paul VI (1975) *Evangelii Nuntiandi*, Bombay: St Paul Publications.

John Paul II (1990) *Redemptoris Missio*, Delhi: CRI Secretariat.

CHAPTER 2

Protestant Mission Trends in India

F. Hrangkhuma[*]

I. Introduction

In the nineteenth and early part of the twentieth centuries, the Protestant understanding of Christian mission was fairly straightforward with a popular theme, "the evangelization of the world in this generation". The goals of mission then were dominantly the winning or conversion of the individual heathens and the planting of churches, so that the kingdom of God may be extended throughout the world. The methods to achieve this were clear-cut and there were only minor variations all over the world. Evangelism was the supreme task of missions, supplemented and strengthened by social services. The major activities of the Christian missions were the preaching of the gospel by every possible means, Bible translation and the production of Christian literature. Medical ministry and other social services such as agriculture, cottage industries and relief work were also major activities. Social reforms also occupied on important place in several missions.[1] The attitude of most missions toward other religions and

---

[*] *F. Hrangkhuma is Professor of Mission Studies, and Coordinator of Mission Study Programmes, Serampore College, and is the Vice President of FOIM.*

[1] Stephen Neill summarized the five principles of the Royal Danish Mission or the Tranquebar Mission as developed by Ziegenbalg and Plutschau as follows:—

1) Church and schools are to go together.
2) Translation of the Bible into the vernacular.
3) Preaching should be based on an accurate knowledge of the mind of the people.
4) The aim must be definite and personal conversion.

cultures was negative as they were of the devil. Therefore, they had to be replaced by Christianity and Christian cultures, which were largely identified with Western cultures.

However, this clear-cut mission trend underwent considerable examination and criticism, beginning especially in the 1920s. Several factors contributed to the changing mission trends. These include the influence of liberal theologies, the Ecumenical Movement, the rise of the Social Gospel, the two World Wars, the rise of nationalism and communism, scientific technological development, the resurgence of religions and the rise of the Two-Third World churches and theologians. What Walter Freytag said at the last meeting of the International Missionary Council at Achimota, Ghana (1957) before it merged into the WCC at its third Assembly in New Delhi (1961), is still true. He said, "Then, missions had problems; now, mission itself has become a problem" (in Sumithra 1984:5). Mission came to mean different things to different people. The term 'mission' replaced 'missions' while some continue to emphasize 'missions' over against 'mission'; while still others are trying to relate the two concepts. The meaning of the traditional terms such as 'evangelism' and others have changed, and mission priorities, *inter alia*, are undergoing changes.[2]

---

5) At as early a date as possible, an Indian Church with its own Indian ministry (1964:229-31).

About a hundred years later, the Serampore Mission developed similar lines of mission, principally by William Carey and his colleagues. Stephen Neill summarized it as follows:—
1) The widespread preaching of the Gospel by every possible method.
2) The support of the preaching by the distribution of the Bible in the languages of the country.
3) The establishment, at the earliest possible moment, of a Church.
4) A profound study of the background and thought of the non-Christian peoples.
5) The training, at the earliest possible moment, of an indigenous ministry (1964:263).

These are representative of mission principles and points of advance, and in one way or the other, with local minor variations, they were followed by most Protestant missions in India.

[2] Donald McGavran wrote, "The words mission, evangelism, conversion, salvation, liberation, revelation and church, form a major part of the advocacy for

The purpose of this paper is to study the contemporary mission trends among the Indian Protestant Christians and Churches.[3] It may be helpful, however, to note the following points before we discuss the documents.

First, in this age of ecumenism and improved communications that have been reducing the world into a global village, no individual or group can really claim not to be influenced by what happens in other parts of the world. Protestant mission trends in India too, whether fundamentalists, evangelicals, ecumenicals or radicals, are influenced by the Western and international mission trends. So the mission trends discussed in this paper are not exclusively unique to India, although there are some Indian uniquenesses.

Second, the drift of the above classification of mission trends elsewhere can well be applied to India. Donald A. McGavran and Arthur F. Glasser (1983), have classified global contemporary theologies of mission into Evangelical, Conciliar, Roman Catholic and liberation mission theologies. This can well be applied to mission trends in India with a bit of local colouring. Earlier Rodger C. Bassham (1979) described three trends: Ecumenical, Evangelical and Roman Catholic. The Orthodox trend should be added to this. However, as J.A.B. Jongeneel and J.M. Van Engelen (1995:446) point out, there are a number of missiologists who cannot be easily classified within them. They include Stephen C. Neill, Lesslie Newbigin, Johannes Verkuyl, Gerhard H. Anderson, Bengt Sundkler, Eric Sharpe, Mortimer Arias, John Mbiti, and Olav Myklebust. These missiologists cannot simply be classified

---

new mission; but they no longer mean what they have meant for the last nineteen hundred years". In the pages following, he explained what these terms meant according to what he called "New Mission" (1983:53-57).

[3]The original title given for this chapter was Protestant Mission Trends through Official Documents. Unlike the Roman Catholic Church, however, the Protestant Churches are fragmented into denominational churches, and these churches have seldom produced official documents on mission worth scholarly probing. Therefore, the documents selected for this study are ecumenical in nature in the sense that they were products of conferences and consultations of mixed groups among Protestants.

as Ecumenical as opposed to Evangelicals and *vice versa*. Also, the classifications are compounded by the fact that there are a number of sub-groups, with their differences, among the classified groups.

Joseph Amstutz suggested another angle of classification when he distinguished three groups. The first sees mission as God's initiative, the second as an activity of the Church and the third as redemptive history. Commenting on this Jongeneel and Engelen write,

> We would characterize the first of these three groups as the continuation of the "classic" or "traditional" theory of mission, which looks for support in the text of the Bible and perhaps also in Church tradition. Over against such missiologies "from above" one can position "modern" views, which derive the agenda of missiology primarily from the world context and so to speak of mission as "presence" or "humanization", as "dialogue", and as "liberation" (1995:446-447).

Their discussion then follows this division into missiologies "from above" and missiologies "from below". Can we classify Protestant mission trends in India into missiologies from above and missiologies from below?

Another classification of missiologies may be based on the model of the eyes. Jesus said that His mission was "that the blind will see and those who see will become blind" (Jn 9:39). Balaam described himself as "one whose eye sees clearly... who sees a vision from the Almighty... whose eyes are opened" (Num 24:3-4, 15-16). Paul understood his mission as a mission "to open their eyes and turn them from darkness to light, and from the power of Satan to God, so that they may receive forgiveness of sins and a place among those who are sanctified by faith in Jesus" (Acts 26:18). There are those whose eyes are opened and see, and there are those whose eyes are closed, who do not see for they are blind. Missiologies of the blind 'feel' and do not see clearly, always searching for truth here and there. Their concern is always in the present; the immanental sphere rather than the transcendental and the eschatological; always exclusively this-worldly. We should recognize that there is considerable overlapping though classifications and labelling are helpful in clarifying the issues in many ways. The missiologies, both 'from above' and 'from below' meet somewhere and overlap. The missiologies both of 'the blind' and of 'the opened eyes' also converge on many points.

What follows is an attempt to identify different understandings of mission among the Indian Protestants.

II. Interpretations of Mission

C. Duraisingh identified the following types of interpretations of mission in India, based on individual writings (1981:50-71).

1. Mission As Conquest for Christ

With few exceptions, the early Protestant missionaries shared the conquering or winning conception of Christian mission. Evangelism was spoken of in terms of military operations, lines of defence, plans for attack, as if they were waging a war against other believers. Mission was spiritual conquest of the East. In a milder expression, the purpose was spoken of as substitution or systematic replacement of pagan darkness by the light of the Gospel from the West. Duraisingh quoted as an example, the editorial of *Harvest Field*:

> In the case of many a Hindu, the first thing to be done is to empty him. His head is crammed with loads of learned lumber and his heart is the birthplace of vices that the English language will not fitly describe. No man would attempt the subversion of a system he did not to some extent understand... (1981:51-52).

Commenting on this, Duraisingh said,

> Even though seldom we hear such expressions of the concept of mission as substitution, several individuals and voluntary para-church missionary bands and agencies share the same Christological and Ecclesial exclusiveness (1981:52).

2. Mission As Christian Presence

By 1902, the concept of mission as a permeation of society

41

began to appear. It means self-extension of the Church in India through faithful Christian presence. Such a concept is represented by Raja D. Paul, S.K. Dutt and others.

3. Mission As Bringing about a New Quality of Being in India

Just as Christ brought a new quality of life, mission in India is to bring a new pattern of life in continuity with Indian life and heritage. This is another mission concept closely related to the concept of Christian presence, represented by, among others, D.T. Niles and P. Chenchiah. The latter wrote:

It is difficult for life to operate across communal barriers. A Christian movement within Hinduism without its umbilical (*sic.*) cord being cut is a decided advantage to the Hindu and Christian.

Duraisingh commented that the resultant new life through mission is beyond communal boundaries since it is a Christian movement process within Hinduism.

4. Mission As Discerning and Witnessing to the Inner Working of the Spirit Everywhere

This is a logical development of numbers two and three above. Duraisingh discerned two shades in this concept. One represented by Devanandan and the other by M.M. Thomas and others. Devanandan wrote:

What we call a particular circumstance in history is constituted, in the main, of three elements. It is the outcome of the impersonal working of nature's laws with factors created by human decisions added to it. However, beneath it all, ruling and over-ruling the ongoing process of history, is the redemptive will of God. There is an abiding value in every passing human condition that is God's secret. At any moment in history, though many things may happen, what is of real and lasting value is this secret intention of God that is shaping the entire process of history towards the final end which God has in view. Only in realizing that presence does man's life at any time gain meaning and significance (Devanandan 1963: 21-22).

The primary task of Indian Christian theologians, then, is the articulation of their faith in such a way that the Hindu who is involved in the inner transformation and renaissance of his faith can discover the redemptive work and purpose of God in Indian life and history (*ibid*.57). Our mission, then, is articulating "the relevancy of the Christian message in (the) very crisis of India's culture" in these days as renewal and revolutionary new beginnings are seen all around us in the life of the nation (*ibid*.59).

For M.M. Thomas, mission is presenting the Gospel as challengingly relevant. He said in 1963, at the Mexico City meeting of the Commission on World Mission and Evangelism,

> Men, whether secular or religious, are asking questions today to which the Gospel is challengingly relevant... The significance of modern secularism and the modern renaissance of ancient religions is precisely that for the first time they are in a situation in which Christianity can participate... It is only as the Christian Missions are patterned to participate in the common agony of articulating these questions and answers to them within the framework of contemporary life in modern man's language, that they can understand in-depth the meaning of Jesus Christ for today and communicate the Gospel of His salvation to others.

To Thomas, Christian mission is grappling with issues of life in the contemporary context, a spiritual penetration into the revolt of the poor and the oppressed and in ideologies.

5. Mission As Search for Community in Dialogue

Representative of this concept, among others, is Eddy Asirvatham in his *Christianity in the Indian Crucible*. Asirvatham called for an understanding of evangelism in terms of a meeting or conversation with other human beings so that authentic community be established between human beings as humans. Dialogue means a living out of our faith in Christ in service of community with our neighbours, and not a secret weapon in the armory of an aggressive Christian militancy.

43

Duraisingh identified a three-dimensional manifestation of the community-in-dialogue, namely,

a) The level of sharing specifically religious experiences in-depth.

b) The level of sharing life-style through structural community living in Ashram.

c) The level of corporate dialogue in and through action in promoting social justice and in building up a community of love and peace (1981:62).

Now we turn our attention to the mission documents.

III. The Devlali Letter

This letter was issued by the All India Congress on Mission and Evangelism in Devlali, January 12-19, 1977, sponsored by the Evangelical Fellowship of India. It addresses the Christians in India.

The letter begins with a conviction that the Gospel of Jesus Christ is "the power of God for salvation to everyone who believes", a realization that God has called His people afresh to proclaim the Gospel to the vast number of the unreached, especially in India.

A series of confessions of failures follows, including spiritual coldness, the failure to work together, the perpetration of Christian divisions, the failure to proclaim the Gospel openly and boldly, the failure to become personally involved in caring for the poor and the oppressed, leaving it to institutions, and the failure to stand for truth and righteousness. It then highlights the great challenge of reaching the millions of Indians with the Gospel, and an appreciation of the freedom that we have in India that provides the opportunity to fulfil the task of mission.

The letter is divided into two major parts, namely "Biblical Imperatives in our Context" and "Specific Actions". The first part provides the missiological foundation and perspectives for the second part.

Numbers one and two affirm the sovereignty of God and the Lordship of Christ as the Author and Guide, and as the one who

44

commissions and perfects mission. It also affirms that "to fail to evangelize is to disobey our Master", and no option is given to any individual Christian and local church.

Number three maintains the priority of evangelism occupying the central place in the multi-faceted mission of the Church in the world. Evangelism is explained as "presenting the Gospel to people so that they understand and face its claims, and calling individuals to repent from sin and to receive Christ as Saviour and Lord". The Letter refuses to identify salvation entirely with the social and economic well-being. On the other hand, as numbers 4-6 affirm, "evangelism and our concern for man and society should go hand in hand. Both are part of the mission God has given us and are the expressions of genuine love for others". Also, "the Church is called to exercise a prophetic ministry, and serve as the conscience of society. We are to stand against falsehood, evil and injustice at the personal, social and institutional levels in fearless obedience to Christ", beginning from the Church.

Number 7 mentions the context of religious plurality and advocates that "inter-religious dialogue based on genuine respect for each other can remove misunderstandings, underline common values and concerns and serve as a preparation for evangelism". The Gospel however is not a negotiable theory of salvation, and dialogue is therefore not an end in itself.

Number 8 affirms the authority, uniqueness and entire trustworthiness of the Bible. The Bible cannot be equated or compared with the scriptures of other religions. "God's acts of redemption in history and His personal revelations in Christ are rightly understood only by God's revelation in the written Word."

The Church is central to the plan of God for humanity. While it affirms the universality of the Church, number 9 maintains that "the chief instrument in its work of mission and evangelization is each local church". This church, according to number 10, should be rooted in the soil, relevant to its socio-cultural context. While maintaining partnership with others from abroad, "mission and evangelization in India should truly be the responsibility of the Church in India". At the same time, the Indian Church is called "to share in the task of reaching all the nations of the world with the Gospel".

The cost of being Christ's disciple should be emphasized in teaching as we are "fellow heirs with Christ provided we suffer with Him". Number 12 concludes with the affirmation that mission and evangelization will end when Christ personally returns in the fullness of His Kingdom. No one "can cause utopia on earth by his efforts". Jesus Christ alone is Saviour, Lord and King.

The second section suggests five lines of action. In "cross-cultural evangelism", the focus is on the 98% of the Indian population who are not Christians, responsive groups should be especially looked for, and new churches planted among them. Families, young people and local churches should be challenged and aroused to do this challenging task.

The section on "Understanding Cultural Diversity" highlights the diversity of cultures, the need to respect each custom and value and, to share the gospel with people where they are. It demands to make use of appropriate cultural forms of communication and encourage those who respond to become disciples of Christ within their own social and cultural setting. It stresses the need to make up for previous neglect by studying, with sensitivity, the beliefs and practices of Muslims in their life situation.

The local church is affirmed as "the key to effective mission and evangelization". The renewal of the local church becomes imperative and this can be done by forming small groups for Bible study, prayer, fellowship, witness and service.

In the fourth section, the call for "effective cooperation" between churches and para-churches and between para-church agencies themselves is emphasized, accepting each other's distinctive ministries, and doing some common project such as research together. It calls for forming an association for better coordination and cooperation.[4]

---

[4] As a result of the Congress, the Indian Mission Association (IMA) was formed. Today, about a hundred indigenous mission agencies are members of the IMA.

In "The Church's Wider Mission", attention is drawn to God's concern for the whole human person in society. Therefore, the delegates determined to identify themselves with Christ in His incarnation and suffering, joyfully accepting humble servanthood. They studied the Bible's teaching on social and ethical issues, the needs of society in India and urged all to be good and responsible citizens, to "expose, rebuke and restrain personal and social evil and injustice in the church and nation". They decided to involve themselves in the local churches to make each a community that cares for "the needs of those around it, especially the poor and the oppressed" and to become the salt and light of the world (*ibid.*).

IV. Missionary Congregations in the Indian Context

The WCC-CCA-NCCI Joint Consultation on the theme was held at Nagpur, October 21-26, 1991, with 45 Indian participants out of 48. The consultation issued a brief statement. Having examined the Indian context from multi-religious, economic and socio-political perspectives, the statement affirms that "God called us to participate in His mission to fulfil the promise of renewal of His whole creation in the context of religious pluralism, socio-economic and gender inequalities, ecological imbalances, authoritarianism and repression...". It strongly advocates the following of the suffering servant of Isaiah 42, realized in Jesus Christ. Becoming one with the suffering should be our mission attitude. It then talks about the urgency of involving women and youth in the decision-making bodies of the Church. It recommends the practice of the CSI's "vision for equipping the local congregation in mission (VELCOM)". It also confesses that the "prevalence of caste-distinction, suppression of dalits and tribal communities, oppression of women and youth in our congregations is a hindrance and contradiction to God's mission", urging the congregations to break these unjust structures. It declares that "God's mission demands the involvement of the congregation in the ministry of reconciliation and healing, in promoting communal harmony and peaceful coexistence".

The statement recommends five lines of action, namely,

a) Exchange visits of regional and denominational churches for better understanding of each other.

b) Facilitate women in decision-making processes.

c) Enable youth to develop skills of writing, arts, drama, etc.

d) Hold love feasts along with people of other faiths.

e) Hold this kind of studies also at local levels.

During paper presentations and discussions, according to the report, an attitude of severe criticism of the past mission mistakes is evident. The Consultation also affirms that the church does not monopolize participation in God's mission; we share this with people of other faiths, because mission is not for others but with others. It defines mission as "God's mission and that we are called to be co-workers with God", the purpose being to bring reconciliation between human beings and Himself and, to renew the whole creation. To participate in God's mission means to communicate God's love to all people and to apply to the present living conditions of all people God's promise towards a new heaven where justice and peace prevail (NCCR 1992:36-44).

V. The Statement of the International Conference on Mission (1994)

At the conference in Hyderabad, during September 19-22, 1994, although "international in nature, the Third World, particularly the Indian issues were taken as the focus". The conference was organized on the occasion of the bicentennial celebrations of William Carey's arrival in India, by the Board of Theological Education of the Senate of Serampore College in association with the WCC. The statement focuses on five issues as imperative for mission today.

In "The Context of Mission", both the global and Indian contexts are summarized, focusing on the dehumanizing structures that increasingly marginalize dalits, tribals, women, children and other minorities who have been generally looked down upon, highlighting the more than 600 million poor people experiencing a survival crisis. It claims to include what the Ecumenical

Movement in its missiological paradigm neglected, namely the growing ecological problems; at the same time it confesses that it has not dealt adequately with "the needs of our women, dalit people, tribal and indigenous minorities, our children and minorities who struggle for identity".

Mission, in "Revisioning Mission" is defined as "God's mission (*missio Dei*) which recreates new communities within the human communities in each place". We participate in this mission by following Jesus Christ, demonstrating love, peace and justice. The new communities are characterized by the affirmation of the culture, land, and spirituality of the poor and the oppressed. There are places that have no discrimination due to gender, race, colour, caste, class and tribe, where death, fear, sin and the groaning of creation has ceased.

"The mission imperative" is "to establish solidarity with fellow human beings, and new relationships throughout all creation" since these are the only means of fulfilling the vision of the new communities. The section concludes: "we are seeking an earth-centred spirituality that is upheld by women, and indigenous people that might be appropriate to Mission in India".

"The Issues" are:

a) Dialogue with people of other living faiths and ideologies, for it is "only in the process of dialogue with people of other faiths that our faith is clarified and enriched".

b) In seeking justice, peace and harmony of society "Christians are encouraged to cooperate with these action groups (other than Christian groups) and where appropriate, share Christian values and visions".

c) Listen to the most vulnerable among us such as women, dalit and tribal people.

d) Serious attention should be given to the growing religious fundamentalism across the world including Christian fundamentalism.

In the last section, "Implications for Our Mission", a few practical suggestions are made. First, the Bible should be reinterpreted to contribute to a new understanding of Christian

49

identity, for developing a counter-culture in societies in which one culture or economic growth dominates and to rethink Christian attitudes to people of other faiths. Second, individuals and communities where God is working should be equipped as part of the mission of the church. Third, Christian education should be taken seriously by theological colleges and seminaries. Fourth, the courses offered in theological colleges and seminaries should be more relevant to Third World contexts focusing on implications of missions amid poverty, exploitation, homeless and marginalised people, and ecological issues. Lastly, the Conference affirms that "God is at work in this world to cause a just social order in which people will experience justice, peace and love". It again reiterates the urgency of exploring the significant contributions the marginalised can make in the new community. "It is in the empowerment of these needy communities that the Church in India may be reborn, by rediscovering its integrity and by beginning to realize what it means to be servant communities participating in God's authentic mission".[5]

VI. The Statement of the Mission-Evangelism Study Project (1996)

This study project by the Thiruvalla Ecumenical Charitable Trust was supported by the NCCI, the South Asia Theological Research Institute (SATHRI), the Christian Conference of Asia (CCA), and the academy of Ecumenical Indian Theology. It is committed to seeking new patterns of mission and evangelism relevant to the Indian context.

The "Statement" was issued by the participants of a workshop on "Mission and Evangelism in India: A Historical Appraisal". The Statement is divided into three parts:

a) "Theological and Historical Perspective of Mission and Evangelism", further subdivided into "Message", "History of Mission and Evangelism", "Context", "Issues" and "New Directions".

---

[5] See for the full text of the Statement and my critical review of it in *Indian Journal of Theology*, Vol. 37, No.1, 1995, pp. 68-75.

b) "Dalit Perspective of Mission and Evangelism", subdivided into the "Mission of the Church", "Dalitizing the Church".

c) "Women's Perspective", with its implications for mission.

Since no new significant issue is added to the previous documents, a few quotations will suffice: "Mission is a response to the promise of New Life in Jesus Christ — a life that overcomes all forces of death expressed as self-centredness, social oppression and economic injustice". In the dalit perspectives "We recognize political involvement in defence of justice and human dignity as a form of Christian mission". In dalitizing the Church, "the mission today is to be part of the despised and the broken". For the dalits, "conversion to Christ need necessarily lead to a new understanding of our Christian identity. The dalit perspective of conversion is the celebration of our identities in Christ as the primary identity, thus fulfilling and transforming the dalit identity itself".

Women's liberation issues should be given serious ethical and theological consideration. "Women have seen as part of their mission and proclamation to protest against such misinterpretations of the Gospel (i.e., from a patriarchal perspective) and to present their understanding of Gospel values". The Church's mission is to give full support to and endorse this.

VII. Conclusion

Two major mission trends are represented in this paper. The first is represented by Duraisingh's first reflection, "mission as conquest for Christ", and the Devlali Letter. The second is represented by the rest — Duraisingh's numbers 2-5 and the three documents. All the minor mission trends of the Protestant Christians in India may be grouped into these two major trends at different levels. A brief comparative study may be helpful.

The first major trend insists that all missiological considerations should start from the word of God in the Bible. God's message in the Bible must speak to the context. The second trend begins its missiological consideration from contemporary context. The Bible is to be reread from the perspectives of contemporary context. Hence the first trend may be called 'Missiology from above', whereas the second is 'Missiology from below'.

51

The most prominent reality for the adherents of the first trend is what we might call eternal, spiritual and supra-cultural reality. This is characterized by the lostness of individuals, emphasizing the salvation of souls and new birth as the entry point into the kingdom of God. It is a spiritual reality in the present tense, awaiting its culmination in the age to come. For the adherents of the second trend, the most prominent reality is the present context. This is characterized by structural sin of oppression, exploitation, injustice and the like, emphasizing the liberation of the oppressed and exploited, working towards justice, peace and the integrity of creation. By destroying evil social structures and working towards producing a just society, they emphasize the reality of the kingdom of God now, in the present. The future culmination of the kingdom concept is somewhat fuzzy.

The major focus of the first trend is the unreached masses of India. This includes everyone without Christ — rich and poor, women, children, tribals and dalits. It emphasizes their spiritual liberation, that is conversion, and their incorporation into local churches in harmony with local culture as far as biblically viable, transforming society and thereby extending God's kingdom. The adherents of the first trend firmly believe that the gospel is God's power for the salvation of everyone who believes. It is also the primary transformer of society. Therefore, without the dynamic preaching of the gospel centred in Jesus Christ, there can be no true liberation. Accordingly, attempts at socio-economic liberation of the poor, oppressed, exploited and marginalized apart from evangelism are not Christian mission. As a result the socio-economic liberation of the down-trodden and ecological concerns, which are taken more and more seriously, nevertheless are always secondary to spiritual liberation. Moreover, the temporal benefits of the gospel are always secondary to the eschatological benefit of eternal life. The transcendental, supracultural and eschatological dimensions are stressed.

The adherents of the second trend have the dalits, tribals, women, children — all the marginalized — as the primary mission focus. The emphasis is on liberation, mostly in the sense of earthly, social, economic, racial and political liberation, to give them a just society where evil structures are destroyed. Involvement in social and political actions and religious dialogue are the primary means of mission, with the purpose, not of religious conversion, but a better understanding, mutual sharing, and harmonious, peaceful co-existence. Church planting is frowned upon, but resultant new communities are suggested without clear-cut guide lines as to the form, character and identity of the new communities. Its spirituality is earth-centred, and its focus this-worldly and contextual. The mystical and eschatological dimensions of salvation are obscured. Social, economic, political, racial, gender, and ecological dimensions seem to comprise true spirituality.

The first trend emphasizes the individual personal dimension of salvation while the transformation of society is emphasized by the second trend. The first trend is mildly critical of the past missionary movements, emphasizing their positive contributions over against their mistakes. Their negative criticism generally revolves around the western missionaries' cultural imperialism, and to some extent, their close identification with colonialism. The second trend is extremely critical of the missionaries' relationship with colonialism, their cultural imperialism and triumphalistic attitudes, almost completely over-shadowing the missionaries' positive contributions.

Generally, the adherents of the first trend are exclusivists, insisting that only in Jesus of the Bible is there salvation. Most of the adherents of the second trend are inclusivists in the sense that salvation is only in Jesus, but not necessarily of the Bible alone. Some are pluralists in the sense that in all religions there is salvation.

Both trends stress a holistic concept of mission. However, their models of holism seem different. At least some of the adherents of the first trend describe holistic mission in terms of meeting the entire needs of a person, that is, body, mind and soul. The socio-economic dimension, as well as ecological dimensions are secondary. The second trend uses the model of justice, peace and the integrity of creation, but the personal, individual dimension is fuzzy.

Obviously, the brief summary above cannot do justice to both the trends and their sub-trends. There are considerable points of convergence between the two major trends. However, the world-views upon which the adherents of both trends build their concepts of mission are different. It is imperative that these two trends meet in dialogue.

References

Bassham, Rodger C. (1979) *Mission Theology 1948-1975: Years of Worldwide Creative Tension — Ecumenical, Evangelical and Roman Catholic*, Pasadena: William Carey Library.

Duraisingh, C. (1981) "Mission Yesterday and Today: Reflections on Missiological Thinking in India" in *Our Common Witness: Report of a Consultation Jointly Sponsored by the Catholic Bishops' Conference of India and the National Council of Churches in India*, Alwaye, October 16, 1980.

All India Congress on Mission and Evangelization (1977) *Go Forth and Tell: Report of the All India Congress on Mission and Evangelization*, Devlali, January 12-19, 1977.

Evangelism Study Project (1996) *Mission and Evangelism in India: A Historical Appraisal*, Madras, Mission and Evangelism Pamphlet No.1.

Neill, Stephen C. (1964) *History of Christian Missions*, London: Penguin.

NCCR (1992) Vol.CXIII, No.1, January, pp. 36-44.

Sumithra, Sunand (1984) *Revolution as Revelation*, New Delhi: TRACI.

Verstraelen, F.J., A. Camps, L.A. Hoedemaker, & M.R. Spindler (1995) *Missiology — An Ecumenical Introduction: Texts and Contexts of Global Christianity*, Grand Rapids: Eerdmans.

CHAPTER 3

Mission as Social Concern —
In Official Church Documents and
Recent Missiological Literature

Joseph Mattam*

I. Introduction

For many centuries mission was understood primarily as the expansion of the Church, mostly by verbal proclamation of the Gospel leading to baptism. Even today some think of the mission in these terms. For such persons, the main concern is the eternal salvation of the soul; socio-cultural, temporal, earthly realities are outside the scope of evangelization. However, during recent years there has been a massive shift from this to a more holistic understanding of mission with the social, human existence in its totality as the focus of attention. In this paper I shall examine 1) the factors that led to a rethinking in the understanding of mission in the official documents of the Catholic Church, in the Catholic Bishops' Conference of India (CBCI) and The Federation of Asian Bishops' Conference (FABC), and other theological developments in the last 3 or 4 decades. Then 2) I shall attempt to describe how the social dimension is presented in recent thinking on mission. I have limited myself to the official teaching of the Catholic Church; though I refer to many modern authors, my primary focus is the

* Joseph Mattam, a professor of theology at Vidyajyoti and other theological colleges, is presently the Director of the Gujarat Jesuit Regional Theologate. He is a member of the EATWOT, IAMS, ITA and FOIM.

published and mostly unpublished writings of Samuel Rayan, a Catholic theologian, whose position is very typical of the social thrust in mission.

II. The Evolution in the Official Teaching of the Church

1. Roman Documents

I shall merely point out some documents that have paved the way for a new understanding. The Communist Manifesto had appeared already in 1848 and the first volume of Das Kapital in 1867 voicing concern for the working class and calling attention to the inhuman conditions in which many lived. There had been a new ferment in European society. But the Church was slow to respond to the human and social situations and develop a social consciousness. For one thing, during many centuries the Church had looked upon social structures as part of nature, like the 'natural law'; even slavery was accepted as natural; it took the Church very long to see these structures as human creations that needed change. There was another obstacle to its seeing and acting on these problems. Sufferings were to be borne with patience as part of "satisfaction for sins". Divine justice, understood very legalistically and juridically, demanded suffering in order to vindicate itself. This view has had the effect of deadening our sense of justice with regard to the oppressed masses. Christians preferred to tolerate rather than challenge injustices. The individualistic understanding of sin, the preoccupation with the salvation of souls and the inner struggles made the Church neglect the larger social issues (Lobo 1981:784). However, the Church could not continue in its slumber for ever, and finally woke up with *Rerum Novarum* (1891). This was an attempt to respond to the human situation of suffering and misery. Though not very great by today's standards, it was a real breakthrough for the Church. Subsequent Encyclicals and some of the documents of Vatican II touching on one or other aspect of the human situation, have travelled a long way from *Rerum Novarum*; they have moved away from its triumphalistic language to a language of dialogue and compassion. The change in the language and emphasis in these documents is remarkable. We may mention the following as having contributed to this change. *Quadragesimo Anno* (1931) *Mater et Magistra* (1961), *Pacem in Terris* (1963), *Gaudium et Spes* (1963), *Populorum Progressio* (1967), *Octogesima Adveniens* (1971), *Evangelii Nuntiandi* (1975), *Laborem Exercens* (1981), Documents of the Pontifical Commission for Justice and Peace.

The documents from Rome showed progressively their awareness of the problems facing humans and saw clearly that the Church had a role to play in these situations. Recent documents begin to speak also of structural and social sins and the need for structural transformation. These Encyclicals and the Vatican II documents, especially *Gaudium et Spes* have in no small way helped to broaden the concept of mission and, partly at least, move away from the triumphalistic, colonialist concept of mission and the preoccupation with 'saving souls'. Summing up a study on these documents, George Lobo concludes:

"From the teaching of the Magisterium, it is clear that development and liberation are constitutive elements in the preaching of the Gospel and the salvific mission of the Church. Failure to... take an active part in this struggle for justice would be a betrayal of one's Christian calling" (Lobo 1981:804).

The birth of the Feminist, Black, Asian and South American Liberation Theologies also had much to contribute to a rethinking on mission. These theologies saw the Church as a movement in the service of the Kingdom of God and not primarily as an institution of power. *Gaudium et Spes* 42 and 43 also supported these assumptions. These theologies forced the Church to look at its mission from the point of view of the downtrodden masses. Though at first Rome did resist these movements[1], now it has come to acknowledge their positive contribution. John Paul II has very clearly shown his support for this trend in theology[2]. The

[1] Instruction on Certain Aspects of the "Theology of Liberation", Sacred Congregation for the Doctrine of the Faith, Rome, 1984.

[2] "Make appropriate responses to challenges of the world", John Paul II's letter to Brazilian Episcopal Conference, in L'Osservatore Romano, 28 April 1986. There he says: "The theology of liberation is not only timely, but also useful and necessary", p. 7.

Conference of the Bishops of South America at Medellin (1968) gave a boost to the social thrust of the Gospel; in their meeting at Puebla (1979), in spite of the efforts of Rome at the preparatory stage to reverse the trend of Medellin, has to a certain extent preserved its thrust (Rayan 1980a:200-216), which is definitely geared to justice and the cause of the poor.

Like the influence of liberation theologies, an event that affected the Church's thinking very radically was the 32nd General Congregation of the Jesuits in 1974 with its emphasis on faith and justice and the option for the poor. These slogans have been picked up by many religious congregations in subsequent years. Also the official Church thinking has been much affected by this and the following General Congregation 33 (1983) and 34 (1995) and their documents.

Even though by and large the official documents have accepted the importance of working for justice, tension between preaching the Gospel and human development has been going on. Some asked: must we evangelize or civilize? Is there no danger of confusing the working for a more just society with the radical newness of the Kingdom coming only from grace and the redemptive action of God? Even though nobody had actually equated mere human progress with the final Kingdom, the Roman documents harp on this even today.

2. Catholic Bishops' Conference of India (CBCI)

The changes taking place globally and in the Catholic Church had its effect also on the CBCI and FABC. Before Vatican II the CBCI had come to insist upon the need for social work, even if for its own survival. In the bishops' view,

> Social work is to be seen as a practical condition for missionary work. Without some form or other of social involvement, missionary work is "inconceivable". Social works are also a *preparation* for missionary work, for these works dispose well the minds of the people and win their sympathy for Christianity (Wilfred 1981:839).

Whatever be the motive, after Vatican II the CBCI felt that more "organised efforts on our part are absolutely necessary".

Western agencies stepped in with large funds, and massive developmental activities were launched. Caritas India was set up in 1960 to enable the Church in India to get the credit for the charitable works undertaken by the 'Catholic Relief Services'.

The Bangalore All India Seminar (1968), Theological Conference of Nagpur (1971) and the Patna Consultation on Evangelization (1972) gave further impetus to this growing awareness of the CBCI. Hence, in their meeting in Calcutta 1974 they saw evangelization in the background of the social reality of India. They called for an evaluation of our educational apostolate among the elite (I wonder if this has ever been done!) and the strengthening of our work for the poorer classes. The CBCI Mangalore 1978 spoke of healing unjust and oppressive structures as part of the Christian search and involvement for a just society. However, as in the Roman circles, some bishops began to be more cautious about the emphasis on the social thrust. So in Ranchi (1979) the bishops said: "Development should not be considered an end but a means. It was felt that today social works and liberation were being overstressed and there was little effort to present authentic Christ through these activities" (Wilfred 1981:858).

This hesitation and caution does not smother the flame of social concern in the CBCI documents. In more recent documents the dalits, tribals, women, ecological and caste concerns receive great attention from the bishops. The recent Consultation in Poona 1994 has clarified many of the issues (Kanjamala 1995). The CBCI has accepted more explicitly that working for the betterment of dalits, tribals and women is evangelization and these efforts need further strengthening. The CBCI in its latest General Body Meeting, 13-21 Feb 1996, shows that social concern is very much alive in its preoccupations. The Report of the Secretary General under the heading "The Major Concerns", reads: "Making the Dalit issue very much alive with the cooperation and support of all Bishops, Religious and Lay Organizations and other Christian Churches" (CBCI 1996:18). Again the section, "Ongoing Thrust of the CBCI" has this: "to give unstinted support to the multipronged strategies to empower the Dalit Christians to demand the statutory benefits which are denied to them" (*ibid* 20).

The guidelines given by the bishops for the last elections also reveal their priorities. Talking of the qualities to be looked for in the parties, the CBCI said that, among other things, they should have a preferential bias towards the poor, especially the dalits, the tribals, the economically underprivileged, the women, children, aged and disabled (*ibid* 84). All these show that the CBCI has not only kept its social concern alive but also has in fact widened its scope to more areas than in the past, for example, women, ecology and more particularly the dalit issues.

Just as the General Congregation 32 of the Jesuits affected the thinking in the Church, in India, a letter of the Indian Jesuit Provincials on Evangelization addressed to their men in the field also had a certain impact on the practice and thinking on the missions. While the letter was to reassure the missionaries of the necessity of continuing to proclaim Christ, the letter is "weighted on the side of justice. Though addressed to men in the field of direct preaching, there is such an emphasis on justice, dignity, humanization and conscientization that it is possible to read the letter as a reinterpretation of what preaching really means in our concrete history" (Rayan 1980b:245).

3. The Federation of Asian Bishops' Conference (FABC)

One of the major emphases of the Federation of Asian Bishops' Conference (FABC), which came into existence in 1970, has been the option for the poor — becoming a Church of the poor. The fifth Plenary Assembly held at Bandung, Indonesia in 1990 came to an integral understanding of mission, directed to the total situation of Asia with all its challenges and with Jesus Christ as the motivating force.

> Therefore mission includes: being with the people, responding to their needs, with sensitiveness to the presence of God in cultures and other religious traditions, and witnessing to the values of the kingdom through presence, solidarity, sharing and word. Mission will mean a dialogue with Asia's poor, with its local cultures and with other religious traditions (Wilfred 1991:303).

4. Missiological Literature

This official shift of the Church from a mere verbal procla-mation to bring about the expansion of the Church to a genuine concern for the human in its totality was facilitated by many theo-logians who had already moved from the old understanding to a more holistic approach to evangelization.

a) Critique of the old: The older approach to missions was in terms of 'foreign missions', of geographical locomotion, con-quest, adventure and martyrdom; the missions were triumphalistic, associated with colonial rulers, full of manipulative rhetoric, un-concerned about the struggles of the earth, with the emphasis on saving souls and relief work (Rayan 1994). There is a growing awareness of the various forms of man made injustices prevalent in the world in the economic, social, political and even religious spheres; these had always been visible but to a certain extent they were explained away as 'natural', 'God-willed', as 'punishment' for our sins, etc., and the human responsibility in causing and changing these situations was not taken seriously. This type of understanding prevailed because for many centuries a dualistic thinking (the natural/supernatural, earthly/heavenly, temporal/eter-nal, material/spiritual) was kept alive in the Church; the Church's (which in fact meant of clerics) mission was primarily in the sphere of the spiritual, the saving of souls. Behind this was also the exclusivistic understanding of salvation: salvation of the soul was possible only in the Catholic Church. Hence even manipulation in one form or another and bribing were allowed if these led to the baptism and salvation of a few souls.

b) New awareness: Especially after Vatican II and thanks to the better knowledge of other religions, the influence of Marxism and liberation theology, Christians began to realize that the old missionary approach geared to the planting of the Church was not sufficient as it was not genuinely interested in and committed to human life in its historical concreteness and totality. Rayan says, "Mission in India with its ideal of Church extension, its relief services and colonial educational system has been challenged since independence by numerous factors" (Rayan 1974b,c).[3]

---

[3] It must be noted that the ideas are culled from various lectures of Rayan, mostly

He mentions the following factors: 1) The inadequacy of relief programmes with concentration on the victims of social evil, without touching the evil, in the context of the peoples' commitment to nation-building through planned development; 2) Secular ideologies like Marxism which are concerned with justice and human well-being on earth have given to the marginalised a certain measure of dignity, freedom and hope; 3) The awakening of the secular, historical hope as against the eschatological salvation emphasized by colonial missions; 4) A deepening awareness of the condition of the poor and oppressed everywhere and of the forces and processes of exploitation; the realization that all existing economic systems in aid, trade or tariff are all geared to the benefit and profit of the already rich western countries; 5) The memory of the association of the Church with the colonial systems; 6) The memory of the two World Wars which have ruined the credibility of the Christian West and of the missionaries from the West; 7) The revival of national spirit and pride in the newly freed people; their sense of pride in their ancient cultures and languages, religious traditions, etc., which question the presumption of missionaries to 'civilize' the mission lands; 8) In the context of the awakening consciousness of our spiritual wealth, the proselytization from the West which is considered spiritually poor is seen as a new mode of colonial domination; 9) A new awareness of the universality of God's saving grace and the role of other religions in this process; hence a slackening in the zeal of baptizing all and sundry to save them from hell; within a growing sense of history, a new religious horizon is emerging that relativizes the Church as a limited historical revelation of God's saving purpose and plan for the world; 10) Looking at religions also as sociological and human phenomena, people began to see the extent to which these can be supportive of injustices and oppression of people. The role of religious system, for example, is seen in the creation and preservation of caste system in India and the lowly condition

---

unpublished; some are without a year or place reference; Rayan himself could not always remember where and when these were delivered, hence some are n.d.(no date). Since they have precious insights I have used even those without place and date.

of many; how Christianity silently, if not actively, supported colonialism and the slave trade for the sake of the possible help for mission expansion; 11) The concept of God that religions imparted led to a type of passivity in the face of atrocious human conditions. For instance, the idea of God Christianity projected down the centuries had little in common with what Jesus had revealed; the Christian God was more a replica of the Roman emperor, inaccessible, requiring both heavenly and earthly mediators, whimsical, paternalistic and supportive of the rich and powerful. Such a paternalistic God-image encouraged passivity and passive suffering (Mattam 1983:497); 12) The awareness of the unity of God's plan and purpose beginning with the first gift of life (creation) which contains the promise of all subsequent gifts also has forced the Church to rethink its mission in a more holistic sense, and see it as serving humanity in its concrete historical conditions. Hence the earth and its produce, its use and distribution as meant for all, became part of the mission of the Church.

13) Rayan refers over and over again to the theme of the mission texts in the New Testament. He holds that Matthew 28:18ff and Mark 16:15f alone are not enough; there are other mission mandates that need to be taken seriously. He claims that even these have been interpreted too narrowly. For example, Matthew 28:18f invites the hearers to "make disciples of the nations", which is more than a water baptism and the teaching of some doctrines. The saving truths that people need to know are much larger than a few dogmas. They include the saving revelation made in creation, the Torah inscribed in every heart (Rom 2:14-16); the view implied in Matthew 7:21-27; the fact that God has never been left without witnesses (Acts 14:17); the theology of Acts 17:16, 22-23 and the teaching of Hebrews 11:6,13 that the faith, without which it is impossible to please God, has existed from the beginning. Salvation is a larger divine project than is envisioned by an exclusivist Christian interpretation. "The suggestion that God provides for peoples' salvation only with the life and death of Jesus of Nazareth is unfair to God, too narrow for biblical perspectives, and too inept for a Spirit-led history of over two million years" (Mojzes 1990:136). 'All nations' may have meant all the Jewish

diaspora. However, even if these words are taken literally as "all nations", what is demanded is the baptism of the cultures and making disciples which is transforming the nations, their culture, their outlook and way of life by the Gospel.

In Mark 16:15f the instruction is to invite people to believe in the good news of God's love.[4] Those who do not believe are condemned. Baptism itself needs to be understood in a broader sense; even for Jesus his water baptism looked to another which he had to receive and undergo as a result of his commitment to the Kingdom: his death. What is demanded is rather the commitment to the cause of the Kingdom and the readiness to give even one's life for that cause. Other mission commands of the New Testament are equally important, as we shall see in the next section.

14) Another factor that led to a new understanding of mission is the re-reading of the Bible from the point of view of the poor and the oppressed. This led to the suspicion that earlier interpretations were class biased, in favour of the higher classes; and to the discovery that the Bible was the story of slaves liberated from slavery by God, and hence only from the point of view of the poor and oppressed could it be properly interpreted.

III. A New Concept of Mission

These and similar concerns led modern authors to a new concept of mission. One is aware that today there is everywhere the slogan that "mission is not to be ecclesial centred but Kingdom centred"; perhaps this needs to be made more precise.[5] Samuel Rayan emphasizes the social angle, though he does not leave out the cultural and the religious.

---

[4] This may have reference to the beginning of Mark's gospel where he announces the Kingdom and asks for belief in the good news and repentance. It is this good news that enabled Jesus to be an exceptional person, fully free and fearless, free from the outlook of the world, from its competitive pattern and could opt for the poor and the rejected of society.

[5] M. Amaladoss, for instance, talks of the aim of mission as "creating a counter culture"; it looks to a cultural transformation, "a change of peoples' world views and systems of values. The roots of such a cultural transformation will be a spirituality that motivates, inspires, and enables people to search for a fuller life

1. The Unity of the Plan of God

One of the basic principles behind the new approach is the unity of all things, the unity of the plan of God: the unity of source and goal. The dichotomy between the natural and the supernatural has to be transcended and reality ought to be looked at as one, for in Jesus such a oneness has been achieved. Most of the mission theology of the past suffered from the valid distinction between grace and nature, the religious and the secular, the spiritual and the material and the salvation of the soul and the needs of the body (Rayan 1971:35f). The Church chose the first of these pairs as its proper domain of mission, with the consequent opposition between evangelization and development, etc. The social and temporal dimension of Jesus' ministry was obscured and hence a new approach to the missions takes these two not as separate but merely as dimensions of the one reality, one world which God so loved and sent his Son to save.

2. A New Concept of Mission Territory

The dichotomized view of reality made us blind to the fact of human life in its socio-cultural aspects which were as much areas of mission as the geographical "mission field". Formerly, "go out" meant a geographical locomotion, transfer to foreign lands. Samuel Rayan is very consistent in showing that the mission area is not a geographical matter but areas of human life that are still not sufficiently transformed by the values of the Kingdom: our politics, social relations, trade relations, economic structures which leave the majority in poverty and misery. The mass communications, culture in general are all mission territories. The Churches and their pattern of relationships, their structures are also mission territory. The mission land is the world, humankind, human life, "every area of life and relationship, structures, proc-

for all (Amaladoss 1996:1). He holds that in today's world an understanding of mission must arise from the point of view of its victims — the poor, the marginalized and the oppressed. "To be counter-cultural is to be prophetic. It is to challenge people in the name of a vision of what they ought to become, by embodying that vision. In this sense it will always be critical of the present" (p.7).

esses, value systems at work in the world which are not divinely ordained, 'foreign' to the Gospel of Jesus, not wholly formed by love, not totally fraternal" (Rayan 1982:2; 1974a, b, c).

And therefore it is ours to look around and examine and study the structures and the value systems in the present pattern of life, national life, group life, Church life, international relationship — economic, political, military. And ask ourselves where people are enslaved, who are the Pharaohs of today, where do we find the Egypt of our day, and what God is saying to us out of the existing, flaming socio-political situations (Rayan 1982).

In his talk at Cincinnati he invites the listeners to hear the call of God from the human situations that need liberation. "God is calling out to us and bidding us to take off our shoes to get to action for liberation, for struggle against the great Lords, the great powers that keep God's people in chains and oppressed. This becomes a major concern from the days of Moses, from very ancient days to the days of Jesus, to our day" (*ibid.*). The Kingdom dimension points to the need of liberation from open or subtle manipulation, the need for justice in social life.

3. Be Light, Salt, Leaven and Fragrance:
Mt 5:13,14; 2 Cor 2:14-16

The early Church saw mission as being light, salt, leaven and fragrance (Rayan 1982; Mojzes 1990). Rayan suggests that we add "draw" to the command "to go". "Go and draw". The newness brought about by the transforming power of the Gospel is what 'draws' people to Jesus and his message. Matthew's invitation to be light, salt and leaven are as much mission commands as Matthew 28. These images ask us to be non-conformists, being different from the surroundings, being salt. Being light is something that cannot be ignored, but will be noticed, precisely because of the new type of life that is lived by the disciples. 2 Corinthians 2:14-16: Christians are presented as fragrance which Christ offers to God and which God makes use of in order to broadcast knowledge of himself. Along with the mandate to be the salt, leaven and light, there are others that are important: "go and do likewise" (Lk 10:37), love one another (Jn 13:34), wash one another's feet (Jn 13:14); Matthew 6:9-12; Matthew 5:23-24 and 6:33 — all these are mission texts and need to be taken seriously, not just Matthew 28 and Mark 16. Evangelizing mission therefore transcends proclamation and becomes a witness through life and work. Mission is witness which embodies in dim and symbolic ways the Mystery we call God. The questions that need to be answered are the questions of the victims of the present economic, social systems: what is the impact of your message on our exploitation, oppression etc?

4. The Good News is Relational

The good news is in relation to the situation (Rayan 1994), that is, the good news is addressed to a particular specific situation. Hence that situation with all its frightening details has to be taken seriously. In India, then, one cannot escape to be touched by the widespread poverty, caste untouchability, economic disparities, colonial medical system, corrupt centralised political system and pluralism leading to communalism. Being salt, light and leaven is in a world of injustice, inequality, etc. Hence,

> Salvation and mission and service of the Reign consist in and grow through compassion and responsibility for the downtrodden, siding with the dispossessed and marginalised, commitment to the liberation of the oppressed, striving to do God's will in the economics and politics of daily life, and becoming through such praxis, a bit of labouring salt, a little transforming leaven, small light in God's great world, and perfume that sweetens its atmosphere and attracts. We recall Gandhiji's advice to missionaries to consider the Gospel of the rose which draws people without many words (Mojzes 1990:137-8).

5. Development and Evangelization

One of the major works of Rayan that deals with the question of development in relation to Evangelization is the paper he presented in Rome to the Jesuits' Commission for Social and Economic development Activities (Rayan 1971), where he takes up

67

the theme of rethinking mission explicitly. He asks: In the face of poverty and misery for vast masses of people, the subhuman conditions in which whole continents live, what is the pattern of love and service Jesus is demanding from his Church today? (Rayan 1971: no. 3). He shows that following the lead given by the official Church in recent years in emphasizing the earthly and the human, and the importance of human development, many missionaries have taken to development projects involving a lot of money and collaboration with all types of agents, with the consequent lessening in the time and energy spent in the ministry of the Word and Sacraments, which raises questions for those still interested in preaching and baptisms. Neither *Ad Gentes* nor *Gaudium et Spes* resolves the perplexity of the troubled missionaries, as they do affirm the value of both direct preaching and also of working for development, without saying anything about the relation between the two. Certain theologies too add to the confusion and discouragement of the missionaries. In response to this perplexity various solutions are proposed. In summary (Rayan 1971:9-14):

a) The mission of the Church is religious and spiritual; it is not to be busy with secular and earthly realities;

b) Others see development activity as a pre-evangelization or pre-mission, as a preparatory stage for the eventual direct preaching of the Gospel and gaining converts;

c) A third group sees social action as indirect evangelization and the other as direct;

d) Though the Church documents clearly distinguish the Church's mission and working for the betterment of humanity, and do not accept earthly progress as the growth of the Kingdom, yet they assert that out of this religious mission follows an obligation to work for the betterment of human community, development services flow from the Church's religious task and are of vital concern to the Kingdom — hence the distinction made is inadequate;

e) Paul VI tried to draw together evangelization and development. He held that there "need be no dilemma and the two should not be placed in irreconcilable confrontation. He speaks of coordination, complementarity and synthesis between the two;

f) Lastly, another position refuses all such distinctions; it takes the work of evangelization as a unity comprising the *missionaries' life, work and word*; and the various activities of all people in the various fields are viewed as parts of a single whole. To substantiate this Samuel Rayan studies the meaning of development itself.

Development is human (Rayan 1971:16-34): Development is often equated with economic betterment and transformation which is very important for human development; but that is not all. There are human, cultural, social and political elements to be considered. The true development is the developing person. It is "bettering the conditions of human life" (Rayan 1971:16) for

> Development is not merely a question of abolishing hunger or reducing poverty. It is much more than escape from misery, disease and ignorance. It is a question rather of building up a world in which every person can live a fully human life; a new world in which people can be truly free of every form of servitude;... Development means a new society and a new style of life in which no person, no group, will seek to make progress or profit at the expense of the others (17).

Rayan claims that "economics is by nature social and human". This total human development involves not only production and distribution of wealth, but a new quality of existence. "It is this qualitative change, this improvement of life that makes for development, total, integral and wholly human... Development is human, and the human is primarily qualitative; it is something very special and has to do with faith, honour, hope, equality, acceptance, selflessness, love and sharing" (25). Development deals primarily with the human, and since the human person is the centre of God's concern the Church has no choice but to be involved in the work of human well-being. God's love for the human is realized in the outward preservation and transformation of the world through adequate structures, and also, in an inner renewal of sinful humans through the Gospel. Both are God's activity and the Christian has to be involved in both. Hence the question of development is not something that is peripheral to Christians, but

69

"something which pushes them to the very core of the Gospel itself" (34).

6. Mission is Translating God's Justice for the Earth

"The justice of God is his faithfulness to his creatures" (Rayan 1977). He provides whatever is required for their fulfilment, healing, completion, wholeness and salvation. The sinner needs forgiveness, the baby needs milk and protection, birds need wings to fly — he provides all these and that is his justice. All the time his goal is to heal, to build up and to complete, fulfil and save. "To let a thing exist is also to let it act in its own way and at its own level. And to let it do so and to enable it is part of God's fidelity to his creatures" (Rayan 1977). He provides humans and the earth what they need for their fulfilment through one another. We have to become his providence for one another. Each of us is God's justice to one another and his justice and fidelity work through us only. He sends Moses, prophets and Jesus — all this is his justice; he keeps sending us to the earth to translate his justice into concrete actions and attitudes. Jesus is God's justice in the sense that this is the way in which God decided to share our human plight and to lodge within our human existence the finest of human existence, whereby human history is enabled to become what it was meant to be: open, obedient to God and to the rest of creation. Through this God makes us just, or participants in his justice (see Rom 3:21f). As followers of Jesus, the one who put the downtrodden human at the centre of his religious concern instead of the sabbaths, we stand for a just order and work for a just fraternal order, modelled on the eucharistic community experience (Rayan 1977).

God's justice is his fidelity which provides all that is required for each creature to become fully itself along with the rest of creation (Rayan 1987b:11); and to be of this God, to believe in this God is to do justice; God's justice is contextual and concrete responding to the situation with sensitivity and compassion. What we can do at the level of structural transformation of Asia is mighty little. But what we do can be symbolic. Such a commitment to justice in the name of God is also worship.

7. Mission is Love (Rayan 1993, 1971)

Love is the distinctive mark of the disciples of Jesus (Jn 13:34-35). It is its constitutive factor. Love defines mission (Jn 13:34-35; 15:9-17). Love is central; on it hangs everything (Mt 22:40). Mission consists in persuading people to love God and neighbour; persuading by word, and still more by deed and the lure of a love-full life. Paul puts it as love of the neighbour (Rom 12:9-13). Love means to share, to care for one another, for the disinherited, the marginalised, and the despised in particular. In John mission shapes up as promotion of friendship and selfless love among people; for him faith and love are one. Love is compassionate love, struggling against forces of death and degradation and being responsible for the victims of our distorted economic and political systems (Rayan 1993:3-4). "In brief, then, mission consists in loving people in an exceptional and surprising manner and measure..." (Rayan 1993:4). The Church's mission is to reveal and to communicate the love of God (Rayan 1971:89). This love is neither a feeling nor a word, but effectively meeting the needs of the needy in their total historical context. This love is more than alms-giving — it is working for a more just social order (Mattam 1994:34f). Love is not doing what we believe to be great and good, but what the group of people we work with need here and now. To the man fallen on the road, bringing him the Torah or the viaticum or instructing him in the Christian prayers would not have been the proper response and Jesus would not have said: do likewise. Our loving has to awaken hope in the people, and a hope that enables them to go ahead, beyond, and to be committed to historical projects geared to the progress of the people. The concern is for the total well-being of persons and hence it looks to the formation of communities of true love, a fraternal city, human beings who live in love (Rayan 1971:113f).

In a situation of abject poverty and increasing disparities between the rich and the poor, our struggle should be primarily directed against economic injustice. The acid test of our faith, religiosity or spirituality is how we respond to poverty (Abraham 1996:41).

Commitment to peace and justice is the essence of religious faith. Working for a new society is making our own love concrete and a response to the situation that needs to be evangelised, as it reveals an absence of God in our injustice, poverty, malnutrition (Rayan 1971:84f; see *Mission in 21st Century*).

8. Commitment to Justice and Spirituality

One of the emphases of mission as social concern is that this commitment to the liberation of people is not only true evangelization, but it is also a spirituality — it is worship. Rayan comes back on this theme in many of his works. For many centuries the typical response to the human situation was relief services; this underlies a spirituality which looked at the inhuman situation as something natural and "basically unchangeable", and saw poverty as due to Fate, or the Disposition of Providence, or the laziness and lack of thrift of the poor and nothing was done about the causes of poverty. Another response saw poverty as the result of backwardness, and hence the solution was seen in following the West, the increase of production, more material development and modernization (Rayan 1991:28-29). This response refused to see the present poverty as partly due to the historical causes like colonialism, etc.

A third solution, which works for organization of people and looks for structural transformation, implies a different spirituality, for it sees poverty as caused by injustice with its structures and traditions of exploitation. Here spirituality is understood as response-ability; "to be spiritual is to be ever more open and response-able to reality" (Rayan 1991:22). This demands a serious historical-structural analysis; and the spirituality implied here is seen as "prophetic with a word of liberation to proclaim, illustrate and live out. It contemplates God in historical events and seeks to join him where he is struggling together with the oppressed for their liberation" (Rayan 1987a:10).

This spirituality is based on a God-experience in the midst of the suffering of people and in the efforts to liberate them; it sees God as present and working in the struggles of the people for a fuller life. This spirituality sees God as the ultimate meaning of all, entering human history to dispel forces of darkness and death, and calls for renewal and transformation, as one who wants to liberate people to freedom, to wholeness and a participatory form of life. It is a communitarian and incarnate spirituality, it is honest about the real; it is rooted in what is deepest in human nature. There is something sacred in the struggles for human rights; there is a divine element in it, for the life of the poor is holy as God abides in them (Mt 25:31f; Sir 34:18-22). Our Scriptures witness to an essential correlation between God and the poor, between the imperiled life of the poor and its divine defence. "The condition of the poor touches the heart of God. Thus the life of the poor and its defence are fundamental to God's revelation and to the human response to that revelation" (Sobrino 1985:110). "We meet God most meaningfully within our involvement and struggle for justice and freedom" (Rayan 1987a:10). The spirituality that is born of struggles for the wholeness of people is "a spirituality of hope growing, like Jesus, in the womb of their conflictual history" (Rayan 1987a:11).

IV. Conclusion

It is comforting to observe that by and large, excepting a few pockets, all recognize that out of genuine love, working for the welfare of human beings — even without an explicit desire to baptise — is evangelization: it is the Gospel in action, life witness and being the salt, leaven, light and fragrance of the Gospel. All the rethinking occasioned by various factors internal to the Church and external to it has led us to a more holistic approach to missions; it prevents us from seeing working for people as less evangelical and as merely pre-evangelization. The insights flowing from the incarnation in which the dichotomy of the natural/ supernatural, earthly/heavenly, human/divine, secular/sacred is overcome in the person of Jesus, whose works of healing, feeding, freeing, comforting were the fulfilment of his own mission of announcing and bringing about of the Kingdom of God, his dear Father, have yet to be carried out in our historical situations with greater awareness and sensitivity to the needs of the people, greater compassion in their sufferings so that the liberating word we bring is not an empty word, but powerful, transformative and effective word, the Word of God himself in the concreteness of our history.

References

Abraham, K.C. (1996) "Reinterpretation of Christian Tradition in Contemporary India" in *Jeevadhara* Vol.26, No.151, pp. 35-44.

Amaladoss M. (1996) "Mission in a Post-Modern World: A Call to be Counter-Cultural", Lecture at IAMS meeting, Buenos Aires.

Amalorpavadass (ed.) (1981) *The Indian Church in the Struggle for a Just Society*, Bangalore: NBCLC.

CBCI (1996) *Catholic India: CBCI General Body Meeting 13-21st February 1996, Trivandrum*, George Pereira (ed.), New Delhi: CBCI Centre.

Kanjamala A. (ed.) (1995) *Integral Mission Dynamics*, New Delhi: Intercultural Publications.

Lobo, G.V. (1981) "Guidance of the Magisterium on Social Questions" in *Amalorpavadass*, pp.771-805.

Mattam, J. (1994) *Religious Life Within a Christian Vision of Reality*, Anand: GSP.

Mattam, J. (1983) "The Lost God" in *VJTR*, pp.495-505.

Mojzes, S.P & Leonard Swidler (eds.) (1990) *Christian Mission and Inter-Religious Dialogue,* Lewiston: The Edwin Mellen Press, pp. 126-139'

Rayan, S. (1970) "Mission after Vatican II: Problems and Positions" in *International Review of Mission*, No.236, pp.414-426.

Rayan, S. (1971) *Development and Evangelization — A Theological Sketch*, Rome.

Rayan, S. (1974a) "A New Look at Evangelization: An Interview with S. Rayan", by Jack Wintz, in *St Anthony Messenger*, November.

Rayan, S. (1974b) *Mission Conference in St. Paul*, Minnesota.

Rayan, S. (1974c) "Evangelization and Development", Lecture to American Jesuits.

Rayan, S. (1977) Evangelization and Justice (n.p.)

Rayan, S. (1980a) "Evangelization, Truth and Manipulation" in *Jeevadhara*, Vol.X, No.57, pp.200-216.

Rayan, S. (1980b) "Evangelization — A Letter and Some Comments" in *Jeevadhara*, May-June 1980, No.57, pp.230-245.

Rayan, S. (1982a) *The Concept of Mission*, Maryknoll.

Rayan, S. (1982b) *The Task of Evangelization*, Cincinnati.

Rayan, S. (1982c) *Hearing and Heeding: Mission.*

Rayan, S. (1987a) *A Spirituality for Today*, Bombay: BCLS, Nos.21-22.

Rayan, S. (1987b) "Asia and Justice" in S. Arokiasamy & Gispert-Sauch (eds.), *Liberation in Asia: Theological Perspectives*, Anand: GSP. pp.3-15.

Rayan, S. (1990) "Religion, Salvation, Mission", in S. Mojzes P. & Leonard Swidler (eds.), *Christian Mission and Inter-Religious Dialogue*, Lewiston: The Edwin Mellen Press, pp.126-139.

Rayan, S. (1992) "The Search for an Asian Spirituality of Liberation" in Virginia Fabella et al., *Asian Christian Spirituality — Reclaiming Traditions*, Maryknoll: Orbis, pp.11-30.

Rayan, S. (1993) *CNI Consultation: Towards a Holistic Understanding of Mission*, Delhi.

Rayan, S. (1994) *Patna Consultation for Jesuits.*

Rayan, S. (n.d.,n.p.) *Mission in 21st Century.*

Sobrino, J. (1985) *Spirituality of Liberation*, Maryknoll: Orbis.

Wilfred, F. (1981) "The Social Orientation of the Catholic Bishops Conference of India from the year 1944 to the year 1981" in *Amalorpavadass*, pp.827-862.

Wilfred, F. (1991) "Final Statement 3.1.2, 5th Plenary Assembly of FABC" in *Wilfred: Sunset in the East*, Madras, Chair in Christianity, pp.298-308.

CHAPTER 4

Mission
and a Missionary Christology

Jacob Kavunkal*

I. Introduction

One afternoon as I was starting to write this paper I received a telephone call. It was from Mr Subramaniam Iyer whom I had met only once before. He had heard me on the previous Sunday in the Church and wanted to discuss some matters with me. I invited him to come straight away.

Mr Iyer is a Brahmin convert who is very much dedicated to Jesus Christ and the practice of Christian life. He is retired and his wife is ill with various system failures, but strong in her faith. He participates in the eucharistic celebration daily and takes the communion home for his wife. Iyer's mother was baptized on her death bed and had a very peaceful death. His father approved his son's change of religion. As to himself he had found the God above all forms and did not require any intermediary including Jesus Christ. He had a premonition of his death and had instructed the children not to disturb him at the moment of his death with any prayer or ritual as he waited calmly to pass into that eternal bliss.

Iyer's younger brother, just retired from a successful job, is suffering from chronic kidney failure. His wife approached a pujari

---

Jacob Kavunkal, the Secretary of FOIM, has a doctorate in missiology. He is a regular contributor to various missiological journals and author of many books; he also lectures in various seminaries.

who without any prior information could say that her husband is suffering from kidney failure and that his body is filled with poisonous blood. He has assured her that if the family performs certain religious ceremonies according to the Vedic instructions her husband would be cured.

Now Mr Iyer is in a predicament. On the one hand he cannot allow these Hindu rituals to the god of sicknesses as Jesus Christ is the only God and he would like very much that Jesus Christ heal his brother as Jesus has done for the family in earlier instances. Thus he wants to prevent any Hindu ritual being conducted but wants to bring Jesus Christ into the life of his brother and the family. On the other hand in all sincerity Iyer finds it difficult to say with certainty that Jesus Christ will heal his brother. Then should he not allow the brother and the family to go ahead with the Hindu rituals? After all the pujari knew the situation without being informed about it. His own father found the eternal bliss in and through Hinduism.

To me, Mr Iyer's dilemma is that of the Indian Church as a whole. On the one hand we want to proclaim what we have experienced in Jesus Christ. On the other hand we see the authentic religious experience of our neighbours of other religious traditions, without any reference to Jesus Christ. Should we try to convince them that Jesus is the only Saviour, and win them over to Christianity?

Mission, in the past, hinged on christology in the sense that it was a proclamation of Jesus Christ as the unique and universal Saviour. And this christology was more a judgement on other religions than a witnessing to Jesus Christ. Today's positive attitude to other religions and the admission of the possibility of salvation in and through other religions is seen by many as disloyalty to proclaim Jesus Christ. This paper is an attempt to understand Jesus Christ in this context of religious pluralism and the socio-economic reality of India, but always basing ourselves on Scriptural evidence.

My starting point is my faith experience in Jesus Christ as the Incarnate Word of God. My reflections are in the light of this faith experience. Watering down my, a Christian's, faith in the centrality of Jesus Christ in my life, is not the aim of this paper. Rather I want to make my commitment to Jesus Christ ever more relevant and meaningful in the religiously pluralistic world and in the particular socio-economic context in which I live. At the same time I want to avoid the negative consequences of holding on to formulations that were made in a particular context, which today may help only to defeat the purpose of the mission of Jesus Christ.

Today a theologian cannot afford to reflect from the perspective of his faith and religion alone but must enlarge the horizon of his readership. Thus, though I speak always as a Christian, in my audience I include also followers of any religion and all people of good will.

By "missionary christology", what is meant is the attempt to be open to the activity of the Mystery (Mk 4:11) — Christ in Christian terms — wherever it can be detected. It also implies that no particular christology, reflection on the Mystery, can exhaust the reality of Christ and His mission. And the purpose of our christology is precisely commitment to this mission which is to do the will of the Father rather than saying "Lord, Lord" (Mt 7:21).

II. The Wisdom of God & Jesus Christ

To begin with, Jesus Christ as we have him in the Bible can be understood basically against the horizon of the history and expectation of a particular people, the Jews. At the same time, in so far as Christ was sent because God loved the whole world (Jn 3:16), the history and traditions of every people must be related to Jesus Christ. Christ relates "not only to a particular people's hopes and longings but to all of reality" (Brian McDermott 1993:17).

The Bible itself provides the link between Jesus Christ and universal connectedness and relationship in so far as Jesus Christ is seen as the incarnation of the Divine Wisdom. "The wisdom Christology found in Greek-speaking Jewish communities combines Christology with a strong biblical base and a cultural sensitivity", comments Robert Streiter (1978:41). The ancient Christian hymns such as Philippians 2:6-11, John 1:1-18, Hebrew

1:3-4, Colossians 1:15-20, etc., identify Jesus with Wisdom. St Paul speaks of Christ as the incarnation of the wisdom of God (1 Cor 1:24). He is the pre-existent wisdom, present from before all ages and in creation. Wisdom christology, as we shall realize is profoundly interconnected with a universal connectedness and relationship.

III. Role of Wisdom in the Bible

Recent biblical studies have thrown new light on the centrality of Wisdom in the ancient Hebrew tradition; they have shown the importance of the figure of personified Wisdom, particularly in the books of Job, Proverbs, Sirach and the Wisdom of Solomon (cf. Roland Murphy 1994).

Wisdom is always closely associated with God's work of creation. Wisdom is connected with the whole of creation. It is present with God at creation as a skilled co-worker (Prov 8:30; Wis 7:22; 8:6). It pervades and penetrates all things (Wis 7:24). It renews all things (Wis 7:27). Wisdom "reaches mightily from one end of the earth to the other and orders all things well" (Wis 8:1).

Wisdom is presented mostly in the image of a woman, lady Wisdom, whose primary mode is relational (cf. Job 28; Prov 1,8,9; Sir 1:9-10; 4:11-19; Wis 6:12-11, etc.). Her connections extend to every part of reality (O'Connor 1988:59). No aspect of reality is closed to her. She exists in it as it were a tapestry of connected threads, patterned into an intricate whole of which she is the centre (*ibid.*).

In the Book of Job the figure of personified Wisdom appears in the poem in chapter 28. The theme of the poem is "where shall wisdom be found" (28:12, 20). Similarly in the first nine chapters of Proverbs we find a series of poems in which the Woman Wisdom looms large (1:20-33; 3:13-24; 4:5-9; 8:1-9:5). God "begot" or "created" Wisdom as the first born (8:22). In the book of Sirach Wisdom proclaims that she has come forth from God, born from God's mouth as Word of God. She speaks of her role in creation, of her exploration of the universe and of her sway over all nations. She comes to the earth like the mist, as the breath of God covers the waters (24:3-7). The book of Wisdom describes Wisdom as

God's power and as an emanation of the glory of God (7:25), living with God (8:3) and associated with all God's works (8:4). Roland Murphy summarizes Wisdom as "a divine communication: God's communication and extension of self, to human beings. And that is a great insight the biblical wisdom literature bequeaths to us" (1990:147).

Thus the Wisdom-figure is the one in whom God creates the universe. She sustains all things. She is God's companion in creation, relating herself to all God's creatures and taking delight in them. Wisdom is clearly an important theme in the biblical theology of creation.

III. Jesus the Wisdom Incarnate

The early Christian community identified Jesus with Wisdom and with Wisdom's care for the *oikos*, the household of all creation. "It was this identification between Jesus and Sophia that was to be the bridge whereby the community which believed that God had raised up Jesus of Nazareth came to see this Jesus as the pre-existent one", observes D. Edwards (1995:34). We can detect this identification of Jesus as divine Wisdom in Paul, and in the Gospels of Matthew and John. A number of texts scattered throughout the New Testament, such as: Philippians 2:6-11; Colossians 1:15-20; Ephesians 2:14-16; 1 Timothy 3:16; 1 Peter 3:18-22; Hebrews 1:3; John 1:1-18, etc., are examples of this identification. Since these hymns could have been sung well before the writing of these books we could conclude that the identification of Jesus with the divine Wisdom must have occurred in the post-Easter community. Bruce Vawter has noted that the oldest christology may well be the one based on these Wisdom categories (1973:153-54). These early hymns identifying him with the Wisdom of God, express the community's faith in Jesus Christ risen from the dead and thus attribute to him a cosmic role in creation and salvation. This has a profound significance for today's search for an understanding of other religions in the context of christology and vice versa.

There is a general pattern to these hymns: one who was with God in the beginning, was an agent in creation, became truly human, died on the cross, rose from the dead and is the source of universal reconciliation (cf. Jack Sanders 1971:24-25). Though not all hymnic texts contain all these elements, some of these elements appear in each hymn and John 1:1-18 has the most. Thus in the early Christological hymns we find a theological connection between God's action in creation and the reality/person, who is identified as Jesus. "He is the reflection of God's glory and the exact imprint of God's very being, and sustains all things by his powerful word" (Heb 1:3).

This reality, Mystery/Jesus is the same Reality "through whom" the universe is created. Myles Bourke is of the opinion that this description of the Son as the mediator of creation "assimilates him to the personified Wisdom of the Old Testament (Prov 8:30; Wis 7:22)" (1990:922-23). The phrases "reflection of God's glory" and the "imprint of God's being" are almost a paraphrase of Wisdom 7:26. Similarly William Lane observes that each of the three functions attributed to Jesus in Hebrews 1:3, i.e., Jesus as the mediator of revelation, the agent and sustainer of creation and the reconciler of all with God, echoes declarations concerning the role of divine Wisdom in the book of Wisdom (1991:12).

Commenting on the dependence of Colossians 1:15-20 on the Wisdom tradition Elizabeth Johnson, a feminist theologian, underlining the feminist dimension of incarnation writes: "Not only the general pattern, but precise terms are transferred: Christ is the image (*oikon*) of God, the first-born, the one through whom all things were created" (1986:279).

The prologue of John uses the language of the Logos rather than that of the Sophia. Yet what is said of the Logos is very much dependent on what is said of Sophia in texts like Prv 8 and Sir 24. Raymond Brown has shown how the Logos hymn is structured like a Wisdom poem, and the functions of Sophia are attributed to the Logos (1966:523). Brown is of the opinion that John substituted Sophia with Logos because the latter is masculine while the former is feminine (*ibid.*). Brown concludes his study of the Logos in John saying that Jesus is Wisdom incarnate, Wisdom came among us in specific, individual, historical and human terms (1996:cxxiv).

82

In his first letter to the Corinthians Paul identifies Jesus and divine Wisdom (1 Cor 1:22-24; 30-31) and deliberately uses a language that has a rich context in Wisdom literature, comments Edwards (1995:38).

Apart from these explicit identifications of Jesus with Wisdom in John and Paul, we have references to it elsewhere like Luke 7:35; 11:49; Matthew 11:19, etc. Matthew changes the Lucan version "Wisdom of God" in Luke 11:49 to "I" (Mt 23:34). Matthew puts Wisdom's words on the lips of Jesus. Jesus, thus, is not just a prophet of Wisdom, but Wisdom herself, observes Edwards (1995:41).

Having examined the ministry and preaching of Jesus in the light of the Wisdom literature, Edwards concludes: "Wisdom categories can provide the basis for an authentic interpretation of the life and ministry of Jesus... Wisdom categories (along with others) can help today's Christians gain an authentic insight into the life and ministry of the historical Jesus" (1995:50).

Some of the early Fathers of the Church also have given a christology in relation to Wisdom. According to Origen, Jesus Christ is the divine Wisdom who is the "emanation" of the glory of God. The divine Wisdom that had a cosmic role in creation is now made manifest in Jesus (cf J.A. Lyons 1982:121). All are created in Living Wisdom and thus all are implicitly in Wisdom. In this sense every creature can be understood as the self-expression of Wisdom. God's power has always been operative in the world of creation. "In this Wisdom, therefore, who was ever existing with the Father, the creation was always present in form and in outline, and there never was a time when the pre-figuration of those things which hereafter were to be, did not exist in Wisdom" (Origen, De Principiis I.4, 5).

Divine Wisdom is God's presence and self-expression. God communicates God's self through divine Wisdom. The traditionally prevalent way to understand the Incarnation is in the context of sin. This is only one of the traditions. Here Jesus Christ is seen as the unique Saviour. The alternative is to see the incarnation flowing from God's free love for creation. The incarnation is not dependent on a Fall. It was part of God's original plan. It is the free self-communicating love of the divine will. Wisdom christology supports this view and can help us in our search for the Church's relation to other religions and the whole of creation in a harmonious existence. Hence as Rahner has observed, "we can understand creation and incarnation as two moments and two phases of the one process of God's self-giving and self-expression, although it is an intrinsically differentiated process" (1978:197).

IV. Features of the Historical Jesus' Person & Ministry

It is stating the obvious that we cannot develop a christology separated from the activity of the earthly Jesus. Nowhere in the Gospels does Jesus give us a self-definition. The picture that emerges of the earthly Jesus from the Gospels is in terms of his ministry. Jesus was intensely aware of God as his Father (*abba*) and himself as the Son, God's anointed one (the Messiah) (Mt 16:16).

He was anointed to proclaim the arrival of God's reign. The reign of God was central to his entire ministry and it was equally central to his understanding of his own mission (Bosch 1991:31). The Kingdom of God, according to George Soares, is "his own particular consciousness of mission and his own personal experience of God" (1981:585). When Jesus announces that the Kingdom of God has come, "He is drawing on his own experience of God as 'abba', the dear Father who has declared his unconditional love for men" (598). The Kingdom was his passion and mission. "The time is fulfilled; the Kingdom has come" (Mk 1:14) is the very opening message according to Mark.

Luke summarizes Jesus' mission by quoting from the book of Isaiah in his first public appearance in Galilee:

The Spirit of the Lord is upon me, because he has anointed me to preach good news to the poor. He has sent me to proclaim release to the captives and recovery of sight to the blind, to set at liberty those who are oppressed, to proclaim the acceptable year of the Lord (Lk 4:18-19).

With this quotation Luke describes what was meant by preaching the Kingdom of God. Whatever ideas circulated concerning the Messiah, "he was definitely seen as God's envoy who would restore justice and take sides with the poor and the weak against their oppressors", points out John Fuellenbach (1987:32). Jesus speaks as an anointed prophet; his mission is directed to the poor and the oppressed; it is a mission of healing and illumination, on the physical, psychological, and spiritual levels. Through this text Jesus defines his Gospel as an announcement of the good news to the poor and oppressed (Hanks 1983:52). The first words the Lucan Jesus speaks in public contain a programmatic statement concerning his mission to reverse the destiny of the poor (Bosch 1991:100).

According to some, through this scriptural passage Jesus is announcing the jubilee year and the fulfilment of messianic promises (Ford 1984:61; Kavunkal 1995:37-50). Jubilee was "good news" to the poor, slaves, debtors, and other oppressed persons who could rejoice in their freedom. There was a redistribution of wealth and everyone was put on an equal footing. Hence a jubilee year was indeed an acceptable year to all types of oppressed persons.

The Reign of God "constitutes the articulating axis of his 'theoretical practice' — that is, the privileged instrument for the realization of the process of conversion from the situation of sin to the condition of the children of God" (Antoncich 1993:104). His words and deeds, his life, death and resurrection were all the actualization of this Kingdom. "The concrete content of the Kingdom arises from [Jesus'] ministry and activity considered as a whole" (Schillebeeckx 1979:143). A fundamental characteristic of this Kingdom ministry is its attack on evil. The divine reign is realized whenever evil in any form is overcome: pain, sickness, death, demon-possessions, ignorance, discrimination, marginalization and sin. The arrival of the Kingdom is experienced particularly by those on the periphery of society (Mt 11:5). Concluding his study on the Reign of God in the Gospels, Jon Sobrino observes that "It is the utopia of the poor, the termination of their misfortunes, liberation from their slaveries, and the opportunity to live and to live with dignity" (1993:371).

True, in the Apostolic Church, as witnessed by the Acts of the Apostles, we see a shift from the Kingdom that Jesus proclaimed to Jesus. In so far as Jesus Himself was the actualization of the Kingdom, this shift is not unjustified, though in the context of the socio-economic and political reality in which we live and in the context of the religious pluralism our christology must take advantage of the Scriptural realism. At any rate the christology that emerges from the earthly Jesus cannot be described exclusively in terms of soteriology. It may be pointed out that it is for Paul and later for Augustine and the Latin West that soteriology becomes the point of contact between God and humanity. But in the Gospels we have a different picture. This contact is spread throughout the entire life and ministry of Jesus in so far as his mission was the realization of the Kingdom.

V. Jesus and Religions

We do not come across any instance of Jesus condemning or belittling any religion as such, though he contested the instrumentalization of religion for dehumanizing human lives. He pronounced woes on the evil practices and the hypocrisy of the religious leaders (Mt 23:13f). The Lucan Jesus, while giving a programmatic summary of his mission by quoting Isaiah 61:1-2, conspicuously omits the clause dealing with the day of vengeance to the Gentiles which in turn makes the audience filled with wrath (cf. Ford 1984:60-61).

Two episodes in his life and ministry may be interpreted as the signs of his universal aperture: the baptism (Mk 1:9-11) and the cleansing of the temple (Mk 11:15-17). The former was a powerful symbol of his sense of solidarity with the Gentiles. The Gentiles were invited to undergo baptism by which they were made proselytes. Similarly in the cleansing of the temple Jesus quotes Isaiah 56:7 "My house shall be called a house of prayer for all the nations". Scripture scholars point out that the commercial activity which Jesus objected, took place in the court of the Gentiles, the only place in the temple open to non-Jews (cf. Dickson 1991:33).

There are also other instances in the ministry of Jesus where

Jesus' religious universalism is manifested such as the parable of the good Samaritan (Lk 10:29-34) and his words in Mt 8:11-12 regarding the actual participants of the Kingdom. He does not share the zeal of the disciples to call fire to destroy the Samaritan villages that would not receive him (Lk 9:51-55). Similarly religion and religious practices do not figure at all in his criterion for the last judgement (Mt 25:31f).

These are orientations for us to develop a missionary christology today. Our christology must be a "bullock-cart christology", to borrow a phrase from S. Samartha (1991:116). As the bullock-cart has its wheels touching the unpaved roads of Asia, for without continual friction with the ground the cart cannot move forward, so also our christology must be in contact with the Asian reality, a leading aspect of which is religious pluralism.

VI. Missionary Christology & Other Religions

A Christology that bases itself on Jesus Christ as the divine Wisdom Incarnate can undergird the Christian approach to other religions in a positive way and promote inter-religious harmony without compromising Christian faith in the decisive and universal significance of Jesus Christ.

A Wisdom christology not only interconnects Christian faith with other religions, but also with the whole of creation, for Wisdom, as we have seen, was with God in the beginning and all things were created in her and all were enlightened by her (Jn 1:1-9). Jesus Christ, the Incarnation of the Wisdom of God, is God's decisive self-manifestation so that humans can encounter the human face of God in Jesus (Jn 14:9).

Jesus Christ does not displace other religions in so far as they are permeated by the same divine Reality/Mystery that became incarnate in Jesus Christ. Jesus the incarnate divine Wisdom, though divine, does not exhaust all the aspects of this divine Wisdom, in so far as he was a perfect human being (Heb 4:14), and human beings by nature are limited. Edward Schillebeeckx has spoken of the finite limited nature of Jesus in so far as he was a perfect human being (1990:159-86). Hence we can speak of the universal meaning of Jesus and the historical limits of Jesus.

Other religions participate in the divine Wisdom. They could be described as institutional responses to the divine Wisdom, which as in Christianity, are also mixed with human selfishness and sin. Since the incarnate divine Wisdom, Jesus, is limited and thus does not exhaust the reality and mission of the divine Wisdom, we Christians can learn something from other religions. Hence "the multiplicity of religions is not an evil which needs to be removed, but rather a wealth which is to be welcomed and enjoyed by all" (Schillebeeckx 1990:167). Indeed, in the light of a Wisdom Christology, we can rightly say with Schillebeeckx: "extra mundum nulla salus" — outside the cosmos there is no salvation (1990:5).

This Wisdom christology makes it imperative that the divine Mystery that we encounter in Jesus is greater than the reality and mission of Jesus. Hence, as we have seen, there is a possibility that other religions may have their own insights of this Mystery and responses to it. If so they cannot be unilaterally "included" in Christianity, as Paul Knitter has shown, but rather "all religions could be, perhaps need to be, included in — that is, related to — each other as all of them continue their efforts to discover or be faithful to the inexhaustible Mystery or Truth" (1995:8).

The more we experience God in Jesus the more we realize that this God is a mystery ever more than what has been made known. Thus the more we commit to Jesus the more open and tolerant we become. Hence Amalorpavadass could rightly claim: "The more I experience Jesus Christ, the more I meditate on the Bible, and the more Christian I become the more I am able to see and recognize, appreciate and integrate within me all the other traditions" (1981:126). This is the mystery of the relationality. Since Jesus is the incarnation of the Wisdom of God he is radically relative. We could even say that the specificity of Christianity is its radical relationality.

What the community of the disciples of Jesus is asked is to confess and witness to what the community has experienced in Jesus without making claims of superiority. Such claims were apt only for the colonialistic times. Making comparisons and judgements about religions can lead only to a crusade mentality that has done untold harm to Christianity and its mission. Instead Christians can reach out to others by adopting what Richard Niebuhr calls, a confessional approach, "by stating in simple, confessional form what has happened to us in our community, how we came to believe, how we reason about things and what we see from our point of view" (1962:41). As Paul Knitter admonishes, "with such a confessional Christology and approach to other faiths, Christians can hold to their personal, total commitment to the universal relevance of Jesus" (1985:203).

Jesus, the incarnate Word, is decisive for us Christians not so much because he is the sum total of the divine revelation, "the focus for all the light everywhere revealed in the world", (Race 1982:136) but for what we have experienced in him, i.e., the experience of the light that he has brought into our lives (2 Cor 4:6). The Christian experiences the human face of God in Jesus. For the Christian, Jesus is the perfect manifestation of the divine nature, as love. He is the fullest expression of the divine nature as far as humans are capable of experiencing it. Hence for the Christian love, compassion, service and communion are of paramount importance as they are encountered in Jesus. In Jesus the Christian realizes that the way to God is through the other.

Thus the content of Christian confession is what God is doing in Jesus of Nazareth with the realization that what has happened in Jesus of Nazareth does not exhaust the divine Mystery or divine activity. Such a spirit will enable the Christian "to pass over by sympathetic understanding from his own religion to other religions, and come back again with new insight to his own" (Dunne 1972:ix).

Jesus is to be seen in terms of God's love in action. He is God's turning towards humans as well as human response to God. Our christology cannot be without reference to our total experience of God's world. This will free our christology from arrogant one-sided claims on the one hand and on the other will enable us to appreciate the impact of the same divine Mystery at work in every religious experience.

89

Biblical faith demands that we hold together the following facts: God's saving will is not confined to the Church alone but reaches to all (1 Tim 2:4) and that all salvation is mediated through the Logos (Jn 1:4). The Mystery of the Logos (named Jesus Christ in Christian tradition) is operative in the life of individuals and in religious traditions in which they belong and which they sincerely practice. What is important is not the name in itself but the Reality. As Aloysius Pieris has observed it is not the interpretation of the Reality or the name given that saves, but the Reality itself (1988:133). "Such names as 'Christ' are only a human categorization limited to a given culture. What saves is the mediating reality to which one culture as much as another can decide what name to give: Christ, Son of God, and the like" (*ibid.*). Moreover, it is not the mere acclamation "Jesus is Lord" that saves, but the doing of the will of the Father (Mt 7:21) which we encounter in Jesus.

The fact that the Logos/Wisdom has been actively present throughout the creation provides the basis for a Christian universalism which sees the Word — the divine Mystery , that became Incarnate in Jesus, at work in all religions. This somehow has not been the basic theme of the traditional christology since Nicea and Chalcedon made Jesus unique: "Jesus of Nazareth is unique in the precise sense that while being fully man, it is true of him and him alone, that he is also fully God, the second person of the co-equal Trinity" (cf. Coward 1985:14).

We have to come out of the circle of the redemptive death of Jesus, thereby associating whole salvation with the result of this metaphysical satisfaction paid by Jesus. As long as we move in such a theological world other religions are saved only "somehow" or at the most "in ways known to God alone". We must be open to the Gospels where the death is the result of the ministry of Jesus (Mk 3:6) and the resurrection is the confirmation of the ministry by God. Here the ministry is the key element. Salvation itself is the result of the creation and enlightening process of the Word which reaches all without any borders and limits.

The Christian faith that all salvation is in and through Jesus Christ is still valid, in so far as Jesus Christ is the incarnation of the Word, the Mystery, though the mission of the Word is not exhausted in the earthly ministry of Jesus. The Christian faith does not say that Jesus Christ takes the place of God, but it only affirms that God has placed Jesus Christ — the Mystery — at the centre of the saving plan for humankind, not as the end, but as the way, not as the goal of every human quest for God but as the universal mediator of God's saving action towards people (cf. Dupuis 1995:93-94).

Christians can affirm that the various religions are themselves nourished by the same Mystery, the Wisdom, leading to different types of religious expressions, even as the same water nourishes all the trees in a garden. This does not necessarily mean an equality of participation in the mystery or of the response to it. The Mystery itself is not reducible to any religion, though present in all. Thus the "Christian" faith is one of connectedness and relationship.

Indian Christians are heir to the classical Indian insight which expressed the inexhaustibility of the Mystery that could not be comprehended fully by any one religion, through the example of rivers and ocean, paths and summit. As Felix Wilfred has pointed out these examples are not to be understood through the Western reactionary liberalism leading to relativism of all religions, but as expressions of the inexhaustibility of the divine Mystery (1995:183-84).

The perception of the Mystery working in different socio-economic and climatic conditions cannot be uniform and need not be so. Thus different human responses are possible and valid. It is equally true that no single perception can exclude others but has to be open to others, to be enriched and to enrich, as is the case in every human reality.

What we have been saying amounts to this: a Christian is to be considered as different from the rest of humankind not because the Christian stands in a privileged position with regard to salvation but because of the Christian's mission/service to the world that he/she has inherited from Jesus Christ (Jn 20:18). This mission is primarily that of manifesting the love of God made present in Jesus Christ and which the Christian has experienced.

91

VII. Mission: a Service to the World

As we have said earlier, Jesus manifested the love of God through his Kingdom-ministry which was one of giving sight to the blind, making the deaf hear, the lame walk, cleansing the lepers, raising the dead and becoming good news to the poor (Mt 11:5). Though Jesus did not define the "Kingdom of God" he expressed the content of it through his symbolic gestures like the table fellowship with sinners and outcasts, through the many healings and exorcisms and above all through the many parables and metaphors.

The Kingdom of God meant the transformation of all human structures in favour of justice and the rights of the poor. For Jesus the principle obstacle to the realization of this divine reign in Palestine was the temple and the class structure that it supported (cf. Pixley 1981:72). Thomas Hanks has shown from the Bible that the primary cause of poverty is oppression (1983:3-42).

A missionary christology must enable us to understand who Jesus is and what he did. We have seen how he came to proclaim the good news to the poor and how he was the good news in himself in all that he did and said. This must lead us to a true Christian commitment and praxis.

The presence of Wisdom in the global context does not reduce the significance of the incarnation of the same in Jesus or belittle the church's mission of making him known through praxis. In spite of the existence of this Wisdom "from the beginning", "in the fullness of time" this Wisdom "became flesh and dwelt among us" "to make the Father known". Even as Jesus through his gracious words and deeds of compassion drew the attention of the people to the Father so too the community of his disciples today must be the servant of God's compassion and love.

It is this historical Jesus who provided a social model of justice for leaders from a variety of religious traditions including Mahatma Gandhi. Hence S.J. Samartha is justified in observing: "It is not the unknown Christ to whom Christian witness points in India, but the Jesus Christ who has already been named, known, recognized and even followed by millions at the crossroads of

Indian life" (1982:268). Jesus is relevant to Asia, "not because the bulk of the Asian masses are non-Christians, but because they are poor", underlines Felix Wilfred (1995:163). In effect this relevancy of Jesus to Asia will depend on how the community of his disciples makes the cause of the poor its own.

As M.M. Thomas has pointed out the validity of our christology is not so much the doctrinal orthodoxy as much as its contribution "for a better quality of life and for social justice" (1978:311). We must recognize the presence of Christ in all struggles for justice and in any spirituality that inspires such a struggle. At a time when we are witnessing an "anthropological pauperism" expressed in different forms of discriminations and marginalizations of human beings, an anthropological christology is urgently called for. Jesus who was a perfect human being and worked for the wholeness of life for all humans must enable the community of his disciples to be open to all genuine attempts to humanization of life.

Our approach must be sufficiently open to India's religiosity as well as India's struggle for justice. It does not deny the importance of history or the presence of the Christic Reality in history. The cosmic Wisdom becomes the meeting point of religions as they struggle for justice, for humanizing living conditions and for ecological well-being. The historical Jesus, who laboured among the poor and who announced the good news of the arrival of the Kingdom, spells out the nature and purpose of the cosmic Wisdom. Jesus, thus becomes baptized in the Asian reality of religiosity as well as its poverty, which Aloysius Pieris has described as a "double baptism" (1988:63).

In Jesus we experience that the ultimate Mystery, the Heart of the universe, resembles the compassion of Jesus. It is not that the idea of a loving God is absent from other religions, but what is stressed is that "the idea of an all-loving Heart at the centre of the cosmos is intensified and given concrete content by the faith that God's love was revealed in Jesus" (Jay McDaniel 1995:145). In Jesus we see God is vulnerable, even to the point of dying with us on the cross, that God is forgiving, even to the point of forgiving our most heinous of crimes, that God is a healing God.

Christians must be distinctive in pointing to this love, all-forgiving, all embracing, all suffering, manifested in the life, death, and resurrection of Jesus. Thus they become the salt, the leaven and light to the world. But Christians are not the unique beneficiaries of this love. All humans are recipients of that love.

The story of Jesus must continue in his followers. A christology receives its authenticity from a transforming praxis, proving that, in the story of Jesus, it continues in his followers, the medium of salvation is operative, though it is not the total mystery of salvation — *totus Deus non totus Dei.*

VIII. Conclusion

The Wisdom christology leads us to adopt a global, all-embracing perspective in religions and relate it to the problems that humanity faces today such as exploitation, marginalization, denial of opportunities for the weaker sections and discrimination of every sort. The Mystery, that we name Christ, is universal. That Mystery belongs to all religions and they all belong to that Mystery since that Mystery is operative in all humans. In Christian terminology "the divine Word is the universal agent of all historical divine self-manifestation, even before his incarnation in Jesus Christ, that his historical incarnation transpires in view of its meta-historical and universal operative presence as the resurrected Lord" (Dupuis 1993:243). The universality of this Mystery, Christ, cannot be localized in a point of time in history, observes Michael Amaladoss (1990:257). "The universality of Christ, therefore, includes all God's manifestations in history, while we Christians see a special, even unique place and role in this history for God's action in Jesus we cannot simply universalize this" (*ibid.*).

Because of this common Mystery every religion is relative and can be enriched by the encounter with other religions. In this context Sebastian Painadath is justified in recommending that the challenge of theologians today is to develop an "inter-religious hermeneutics" (1991:287). For all religious scriptures and symbols of religions "articulate in diverse languages God's ineffable Word spoken to humankind" (*ibid.*).

94

The incarnation is to be seen in terms of its purpose, action or operation. The problem is that in the past we have tried to see it in quantitative terms in as much as we asked how far Jesus was God. The divine nature is not a quantity of substantial stuff, but an activity of carrying out a purpose. This activity is love. The Incarnation can then be seen as the case of "inhistorization" of the divine love. It is the divine love operating in a finite mode, it is the eternal divine agape made flesh, historized.

Our christology must be the basis not so much for the justification of a Church that sees itself as the community of the saved, as was the case in the past, but for a Church that sees itself as the servant of a new humanity. A missionary christology inspires the Church not so much to be an institution of salvation as much to be the salt, the leaven and the light to the world.

References

Amaladoss, M. (1990) *Making All Things New: Mission in Dialogue*, Anand: GSP.

Amalorpavadass D.S. (1981) "The Core and Source of Dialogue" in Nambiaparambil (ed.), *Religions and Man: World Conference of Religions*, Cochin, pp.120-135.

Antoncich R. (1993) "Liberation Theology and the Social Teaching of the Church", in Ellacuria & Sobrino (Eds.), *Mysterium Liberationis*, New York: Orbis Books, pp.103-122.

Bosch David (1991) *Transforming Mission: Paradigm Shifts in Theology of Mission*, New York: Orbis Books.

Bourke M.M. (1990) "The Epistle to the Hebrews", in R. Brown et al. (eds.), *Jerome Biblical Commentary*, Englewood Cliffs, NJ: Prentice Hall, pp.922-23.

Brown R. (1966) *The Gospel According to John (i-xii)*, Garden City, New York: Doubleday.

Coward H. (1985) *Pluralism Challenge to World Religions*, New York: Orbis Books.

Dickson K. (1991) *Uncompleted Mission — Christianity and Exclusivism*, New York: Orbis Books.

Dunne J. (1972) *The Way of All the Earth*, New York: Macmillan.

Dupuis J. (1995) "Religious Plurality and the Christological Debate", in *FOCUS* Vol.15/2 pp.88-97.

Dupuis J. (1993) *Jesus Christ at the Encounter of World Religions*, New York: Orbis Books.

Edwards D. (1995) *Jesus the Wisdom of God*, New York: Orbis Books.

Ford M.J. (1984) *My Enemy is My Guest Jesus and Violence in Luke*, New York: Orbis Books.

Fuellenbach J. (1987) *The Kingdom of God the Heart of Jesus' Message for Us Today*, Manila: Divine Word Publications.

Hanks T. (1983) *God so Loved the Third World*, New York: Orbis Books.

Johnson E. (1986) "Jesus the Wisdom of God: A Biblical Basis for Non-Androcentric Christology" in *Ephemerides Theologicae Louvanienses*, Vol.61, pp.261-294.

Kavunkal J. (1995) *The Abba Experience of Jesus: Model & Motive for Mission*, Indore: Sat Prakashan.

Knitter P. (1995) *One Earth Many Religions*, New York: Orbis Books.

Knitter P. (1985) *No Other Name? A Critical Survey of Christian Attitudes Toward the World Religions*, New York: Orbis Books.

Lane W.L. (1991) *Word Biblical Commentary: Vol.47a, Hebrews 1-8*, Dallas: Word Books.

Lyons J. A. (1982) *The Cosmic Christ in Origen and Teilhard de Chardin: A Comparative Study*, Oxford: Oxford University Press.

McDaniel J.B. (1995) *With Roots and Wings — Christianity in an Age of Ecology and Dialogue*, New York: Orbis Books.

McDermott B. (1993) *Word Became Flesh — Dimensions of Christology*, Minnesota: Michael Glazier.

Murphy E.R. (1994) "Wisdom Literature and Biblical Theology" in *Biblical Theology Bulletin*, Vol.24, pp.4-7.

Murphy E.R. (1990) *The Tree of Life: An Exploration of Biblical Wisdom Literature*, New York: Doubleday.

O'Connor K.M. (1988) *The Wisdom Lite2rature*, Wilmington: Michael Glazier.

Niebuhr R. (1962) *The Meaning of Revelation*, New York: Macmillan.

Painadath S. (1991) "Dynamics of a Culture of Dialogue", in John T.K. (ed.), *Bread and Breath*, Anand: GSP, pp.279-291.

Pieris A. (1988) *Love Meets Wisdom: a Christian Experience of Buddhism*, New York: Orbis Books.

Pieris A. (1988) *An Asian Theology of Liberation*, New York: Orbis Books.

Pixley G.V. (1981) *God's Kingdom*, London: SCM Press.

Race A. (1982) *Christians and Religious Pluralism: Patterns in the Christian Theology of Religions*, New York: Orbis Books.

Rahner K. (1978) *Foundations of Christian Faith*, New York: Seabury Press.

Samartha S.J. (1991) *One Christ — Many Religions: Toward a Revised Christology*, New York: Orbis Books.

Samartha S. J. (1982) "Indian Realities and the Wholeness of Christ" in *IMR*, Vol 4, pp. 262-271.

Sanders J.T. (1971) *The New Testament Christological Hymns: the Historical Religious Background*, London: Cambridge University Press.

Schillebeeckx E. (1990) *Church: The Human Story of God*, New York: Crossroad.

Schillebeeckx E. (1979) *Jesus — An Experiment in Christology*, New York: Sebury Press.

Soares-Prabhu G. (1981) "The Kingdom of God: Jesus' Vision of a New Society", in D.S. Amalorpavadass (ed.), *The Indian Church in the Struggle for a New Society*, Bangalore: NBCLC., pp.579-608.

Sobrino J. (1993) "Central Position of the Reign of God in Liberation Theology" in I. Ellacuria & J. Sobrino (eds.), *Mysterium Liberationis: Fundamental Concepts of Liberation Theology*, New York: Orbis Books, pp.350-388.

Thomas M.M. (1978) *Towards a Theology of Contemporary Ecumenism*, Madras: CLS.

Streiter R. (1978) "The Anonymous Christian and Christology" in *Missiology,* Vol.VI/1, pp.29-52.

Vawter B. (1973) *An Essay Toward a New Testament Christology*, Garden City: Dobleday.

Wilfred F. (1995) *From the Dusty Soil*, Madras: University of Madras.

Panikkar, R. (1991) "Dynamics of a Culture of Dialogue," in John
    T.K. (ed.), *Bread and Breath*, Anand, GSP, pp. 279–291.

Pieris, A. (1988) *Love Meets Wisdom: A Christian Experience of
    Buddhism*, New York, Orbis Books.

Pieris, A. (1988) *An Asian Theology of Liberation*, New York, Orbis
    Books.

Robey, C.V. (1981) *God's Kingdom*, London, SCM Press.

Race, A. (1982) *Christians and Religious Pluralism: Patterns in
    the Christian Theology of Religions*, New York, Orbis Books.

Rahner, K. (1978) *Foundations of Christian Faith*, New York,
    Seabury Press.

Samartha, S.J. (1991) *One Christ — Many Religions: Toward a
    Revised Christology*, New York, Orbis Books.

Samartha, S.J. (1982) "Indian Realities and the Wholeness of
    Christ," in *Mis. Vol. 6, pp. 269–271.

Sanders, E.P. (1971) *The New Testament in Chronological Order*,
    Institute of Religious Background, London, Cambridge University
    Press.

Schillebeeckx, E. (1990) *Church: The Human Story of God*, New
    York, Crossroad.

Schillebeeckx, E. (1979) *Jesus — An Experiment in Christology*,
    New York, Seabury Press.

Senior-Prabhu, C. (1981) "The Kingdom of God," in *et al.* Vidien
    (ed.) in Second, ch. D.S. Amaladass (ed.), *The Indian Church in
    the Struggle for a New Society*, Bangalore, NBCLC, pp. 378–638.

Sobrino, J. (1993) "Central Position of the Reign of God in Libe-
    ration Theology," in I. Ellacuria & J. Sobrino (eds.), *Mysterium
    Liberationis: Fundamental Concepts of Liberation Theology*, New York,
    Orbis Books, pp. 350–388.

Thomas, M.M. (1978) *Towards a Theology of Communism*,
    Bangalore, Madras, CLS.

Stranger, A. (1972) "The Appropriate Mechanism and Christology"
    in *Mission*, Vol. VII, pp. 20–42.

Warren, R. (1973) *An Easy Introduction to Christian Missionary*,
    Garden City, Doubleday.

Wilfred, F. (1985) *From the Dusty Soil*, Madras, University of
    Madras.

CHAPTER 5

Ecumenical Endeavour and Mission — Creative Tension

Sebastian C.H. Kim and Kirsteen Kim*

I. Introduction

The rediscovery that mission and unity belong together dates to the middle years of this century. At the watershed Assembly in Willingen in 1952, the WCC adopted a statement on "The Calling of the Church to Mission and Unity" (Goodall 1953:193-200). Since then this intimate relationship has become part of the broad consensus on mission as outlined, for example, by David J. Bosch in his monumental work, *Transforming Mission* (1991). In this paper we shall trace the emergence of this relationship during the twentieth century by looking first at *unity for mission* and secondly at *mission for unity*. By examining Evangelical responses to developments in the Ecumenical Movement, we shall then consider more carefully the nature of the link between mission and unity, which we shall describe as a *creative tension*.

In view of the title given for this paper it is necessary to clarify the use of the term ecumenical. It is true as David Bosch reminds us that "the ecumenical movement is wider than the WCC" (*ibid.*:461). In this paper, however, the terms *Ecumenical Movement* and the noun *Ecumenical* will be used to refer to the move-

---

* Sebastian Kim, originally from South Korea, is a Visiting Lecturer in missiology at Union Biblical Seminary, Pune. He is a member of the Fellowship of Indian Missiologists. Kirsteen Kim, who is British by birth, teaches missiology at the same institution.

ment associated with the WCC. *Ecumenical endeavour* will refer to all efforts toward greater unity.

II. Unity for Mission

1. Edinburgh 1910

It has often been noted that the origins of the ecumenical movement lie in the missionary movement. Stephen Neill puts it strongly, "It cannot be said too often or too emphatically that the ecumenical movement arose from the missionary movement" (Rouse & Neill 1993 [1954]: 362). In particular it had its genesis in the World Missionary Conference at Edinburgh in 1910. The impetus for that gathering was the practical need for further co-operation on the mission field between the various (Protestant) churches and missions. From Edinburgh there emerged a concern for church unity that was motivated primarily by a concern for the world (Bosch 1991:459).

In order to make the attendance as broad as possible (and to include the Anglo-Catholics in particular), theology was ruled out as the subject of discussion at Edinburgh. Therefore no theology of mission and unity emerged directly from that meeting. The enterprise was however justified by reference to various biblical passages (cf. Jn 17:20-23; Col 1:20; Eph 4:1-4).

Three major movements emerged from Edinburgh 1910. The International Missionary Council brought mainly missionaries together. The other two were more ecclesiastical in composition. The Universal Christian Council for Life and Work promoted fellowship between the churches in dealing with ethical issues, while the World Conference on Faith and Order set about seriously examining the theological differences which separated the churches. The latter two came together in 1948 to form the World Council of Churches.

2. The Church of South India

Meanwhile other movements toward unity began on a more local scale. It was here in India where the most dramatic progress toward visible organic church union was made. Stimulated by

Edinburgh (Sundkler 1965:91), a meeting of Indian clergymen at Tranquebar was convened in 1919 by Bishop Samuel Azariah at which a movement toward a broad union of churches was envisaged. The Tranquebar Manifesto (for the full text see *ibid.*:101-102) makes it clear that the primary motivation for such a union was the witness of the church:

> We face together the titanic task of winning India for Christ... Yet... we find ourselves rendered weak and relatively impotent by our unhappy divisions...

The "Lambeth Quadrilateral" was put forward as a basis for such a union.[1] Twenty-eight years of painful negotiations involving the South India United Church (itself a union of Presbyterian and Congregational churches), Anglican and Methodist churches were necessary before the formation of the Church of South India in 1947. The sticking point was not faith but polity. This was hardly surprising since there was no previous example of a union between episcopal and non-episcopal churches. The issues being discussed lay at the heart of the Reformation struggles and consequently became a subject of discussion in the West as well as India.

The CSI was hailed as a major breakthrough. Its model became a basis of the schemes of union in North India, Pakistan, Sri Lanka, Iran and Nigeria (Neill & Rouse 1993[1954]:476). Around the world it was held up as an example, even as the greatest event since the Reformation! As well as the astounding fact that lasting union had been achieved (Sundkler 1965:345), an immediate benefit of the union, as Stephen Neill points out was that Western denominational labels "disappeared" and in their place stood an Indian church (1960:61).

---

[1] This had been defined by the Lambeth Conference of 1888 as a necessary minimum for Christian reunion. *Viz*:

(i) The Holy Scriptures of the Old and New Testaments, as containing all things necessary for salvation.

(ii) The Apostles' Creed and the Nicene Creed.

(iii) The two Sacraments ordained by Christ himself — Baptism and the Lord's Supper.

(iv) The historic Episcopate, locally adapted.

Subsequent reflection has been more sober than the eulogies of the time. As far as its impact on the mission is concerned, J.W. Sadiq comments in 1976 that the church had not become notably more indigenous or more concerned for the nation. And, whereas mission and evangelism were the prime motivating factors for the union, a 1963 report showed that evangelism had come to occupy a minor place and the union itself had contributed to increased introversion (163-165). Sam Amirtham also laments that union has done nothing for evangelistic fervour (1980:85). T.V. Philip argues that the process of reconciling Western denominational polities and confessions did not result in an Indian church open to the plurality of Indian society (1994:106). However, despite the problems, none of these authors suggests that CSI was a mistake — Sadiq categorically rejects such an idea as "blasphemous" (1976:165). But the CSI itself has described its formation as a decision to "unite in order to unite". The struggle towards unity in mission is an on-going one.

India, perhaps because of its unique missionary context, continues to lead the way in ecumenical endeavour. The CSI has held discussions on unity with Lutherans. The Church of North India was formed with the inclusion of some Baptists resulting in an acceptance of both infant and adult baptismal practices. Furthermore, in 1978 a joint council was established by the CSI, CNI and the Mar Thoma Church reflecting a high degree of union: intercommunion, doctrinal unity, episcopal polity, mutual recognition of one another's ministry, and some joint action. Only organisational differences remain (Amirtham 1980:88-89).

III. Mission for Unity

As the example of CSI shows, the impetus for further unity came particularly strongly from the "younger churches". In the non-Western world denominational divisions were resented as "divisions which we did not create, and which we do not desire to perpetuate" (*Tranquebar Manifesto* in Sundkler 1965:101). At Willingen meeting of the IMC in 1952 the delegates from the "younger churches" made this clear in a statement, "While unity may be desirable in the lands of the older churches, it is *impera-*

tive in those of the younger churches" (Goodall 1953:234 — italics original). As Lesslie Newbigin points out, it is in the context of mission, where the gospel is being proclaimed, that disunity is exposed for what it is (1964[1953]:151). In such a situation it becomes obvious that unity is the will of God.

1. The Ecumenical Movement

The realization of the scandal of disunity resulted in a different approach to the mission-unity relationship. The achievement of unity came to represent for many an end in itself, an aim of mission, even *the* aim of mission.

The initial activism for unity was strengthened by theological arguments for seeing unity as the aim of mission. It should be pointed out, though it is not possible to elaborate here, that much of this was already part of Orthodox theology and represented a rediscovery of Orthodoxy either directly through the study of the Church Fathers or through the Orthodox churches, the bulk of which joined the WCC at New Delhi in 1961. The main theological arguments have centred around the new understanding of mission as *missio Dei* which came to the fore at Willingen 1952, the cosmic Christ christology which surfaced at New Delhi 1961, and the renewed interest in pneumatology dominant at Canberra 1991.

a) *Missio Dei* and the trinitarian foundation of mission. Karl Barth is usually credited with showing that mission has its origin in the sending activity of God who is Trinity. Thus, not only is unity grounded in trinitarian doctrine but so is mission. In this way mission and unity become closely identified as two aspects of our understanding of God. Thus Willingen declared, "The calling of the Church to mission and unity issues from the nature of God Himself" (Goodall 1953:193).

The concept of *missio Dei* led to a widening of the meaning of mission. Bosch explains the reasoning, "Since God's concern is for the entire world, this should also be the scope of *missio Dei*" (1991: 391). Under the influence of Hans Hoekendijk in particular, many were encouraged to bypass the church as an agent of mission. Instead they looked for signs of God's activity in movements of history and sought to participate in these. In Hoekendijk's

103

view, mission became a movement of humanization — or "shalom" as Hoekendijk preferred and which he understood as development/modernization. The aim of mission was thus to unite humanity in a modern, secular society, "the great society" which he identified with the kingdom (*ibid.* 382-385,391-392).

b) The cosmic Christ and the unification of all things. The intention of God in sending Jesus Christ to sum up, comprehend, reconcile or unite all things in him, expressed in Colossians 1:20 was the subject of Joseph Sittler's main address at New Delhi 1961 on the theme "Called to Unity". Sittler urged the Ecumenical Movement to a "fuller unity" commensurate with the "dimensions of the New Testament vision" embracing the whole of human history and even nature (WCC 1962: 15).

Sittler's address proved extraordinarily prophetic. At first only the goal of uniting humanity was embraced. This led to the emergence of "the unity of mankind" as a major theme of the Uppsala Assembly in 1968 and the title of a resulting study project. The unity of humankind in WCC thinking has been applied both to socio-political solidarity with the oppressed and to religious pluralism and interfaith dialogue.

Sittler's other thrust toward the reconciliation of nature did not become prominent until Nairobi 1975, by which time the ecological crisis was a major issue. At Nairobi the unity of the church was described as a *sign* of the unity of the whole world, but it was not equated with it (for details of these developments see Mueller-Fahrenholz 1978: *passim.*). But by Canberra 1991 that distinction was no longer evident as Hyun-Kyung Chung, dancing like a Korean shaman, called on the assembly to "participate in the Holy Spirit's political economy of life fighting for our life on this earth in solidarity with all living beings" (Kinnamon 1991:46).

c) The unbound Spirit of mission. A third strand in the theology of mission and unity, which Chung Hyun-Kyung also represents, is a recovery of interest in the work of the Holy Spirit. Harry R. Boer (1961) drew attention to the missionary nature of the Spirit. He argued that Pentecost and not the Great Commission was the launchpad for mission. Thus the church and her mission find a common source in the activity of the Spirit. John V.

Taylor (1971) described the Spirit as both "the elemental energy of communion itself" and also "the Go-Between God", broadening the mission of the Spirit to encompass the universe.

This new awareness of the free activity of the one Spirit in the world has led to suggestions that the *filoque* clause added to the Nicene Creed by the Western church should be expunged because it seems to limit the activity of the Spirit to within the church, the body of the second person of the Trinity. Chung therefore, in the "language of liberation, connection and unification from below", called upon the Spirit to "renew the whole creation" (Kinnamon 1991:42).

IV. Mission and Unity: Creative Tension

The foregoing discussion on unity for mission and mission for unity has highlighted some of the arguments for a close relation between mission and unity: the biblical passages, the practical necessity of unity for mission, the trinitarian origin of mission and unity, the goal of uniting all things in Christ, and the unifying mission of the Spirit.

At Vatican II the Catholic Church made an unprecedented commitment to "the restoration of unity among all Christians" (*Unitatis Redintegratio* 1) and also recognised the close link between unity and mission (*Ad Gentes* 6). Later a joint study paper was published by the Catholic Church and the WCC on mission and unity which brought the two together in the form of the expression "common witness" (Joint Working Group 1984). Unfortunately there is no space to do justice to *Common Witness* in this particular paper.

Mission could be regarded as the "flipside" of unity and *vice versa*, at any rate they are partners for they belong very much together. To neglect either one of them is to lose both (Bosch 1991:460). But all three theological points — *missio Dei*, cosmic Christ and the mission of the Spirit — have been taken further than that and used to imply that unity is the sole aim of mission. Ecumenical endeavour has been broadened to such an extent that it has swallowed up mission. It seems that where we have ecumenical endeavour there is no longer a place for mission. Indeed the missionary movement became an embarrassment for the Ecumenical Movement as evidenced by Walter Freytag's famous remark at Ghana 1957/58 that instead of missions having problems, they had now become a problem themselves (Orchard 1958:138).

Although mission and ecumenical endeavour are intimately linked, they are not the same. It is the thesis of this paper that *mission and unity are closely connected but nevertheless distinct concepts to be related in a positive dialectic.* They are distinct because mission cannot be reduced to ecumenical endeavour nor can all ecumenical endeavour be described as mission. Mission and unity represent movements in opposite directions which should complement each other: mission represents a sending out and unity represents a gathering in. Mission and unity should not be identified or confused but held in a creative tension.

1. The Evangelical Critique

Evangelicals are among those who have sought to uphold mission as distinct from ecumenical endeavour and have been leading critics of an all-embracing ecumenism. In 1974 the most representative Evangelical gathering ever, meeting at Lausanne in Switzerland, made a Covenant which included a commitment to "Cooperation in Evangelism" (*Lausanne Covenant*: para.7).

It must be said that Evangelicals are not known for their unity and for them Lausanne was a great step forward. By their own admission, their "testimony has sometimes been marred by sinful individualism and needless duplication" (*ibid.*). Their paramount concern is for mission, which is understood primarily as making the gospel known and converting as many as possible to Christian faith. Following in the tradition of Edinburgh, Evangelicals tend to come together for the sake of mission, and not primarily to bring about unity. So, though the Covenant affirmed that "the Church's visible unity in truth is God's purpose", the stress is on the missionary motive: "Evangelism also summons us to unity, because our oneness strengthens our witness, just as our disunity undermines our gospel of reconciliation" (*ibid.*). There is a general pledge to seek deeper unity but this is eclipsed by a specific call for the development of regional and functional cooperation for the furtherance of the church's mission, for strategic planning, for mutual encouragement, and for the sharing of resources and experience (*ibid.*).

For Evangelicals, efforts toward organic unity of churches tend to be seen as a distraction from the urgent task of world evangelization. "Organisational unity may take many forms and does not necessarily forward evangelism" (*ibid.*). Short-term expediency and good stewardship demand efficient use of resources to accomplish the task of world evangelization. Furthermore, concern for doctrinal purity leads Evangelicals to reject any compromise which might distort or water down the gospel. Unity must be "in truth" — a phrase which occurs in the Lausanne Covenant, paragraph 7 *twice*. Consequently they have, for the most part, eschewed any organic form of unity, preferring instead the model of cooperation between churches and between church and parachurch (a phrase used to refer to multiple specialist evangelistic organizations).

Evangelicals may be justly criticised for a lack of concern for unity — even a tendency to divisiveness, a weak ecclesiology, and often a rather narrow definition of mission. But they do have a concern for the gospel and for the lost, and a conviction of the importance of mission. Since this paper is written *from the perspective of mission*, we will focus on the Evangelical response to the widening of ecumenical endeavour to show the latter's serious implications for mission.

While appreciating many of the theological insights of the past fifty years concerning mission and unity, Evangelicals have several times registered their dismay at what they see as a tendency to sacrifice mission to ecumenical endeavour. The most crucial points in the debate about ecumenical endeavour and mission were probably the WCC assemblies at New Delhi 1961, Uppsala 1968 and Canberra 1991. In order to demonstrate what is meant by a relation of creative tension between mission and unity we will examine the criticisms raised by Evangelicals at each of these points. These will also relate, respectively, to the three theological considerations enumerated earlier: *missio Dei*, cosmic Christ and the work of the Spirit.

2. New Delhi 1961:
Integration of the IMC and WCC and Missio Dei

By 1961 it was agreed that, in light of the *missio Dei*, the church rightly understood is essentially missionary. Therefore it was felt that independent missions represented a failure of the church to exercise its missionary function. This led to the conviction of many that all missions should be part of a church. This reasoning was the main theological argument put forward at the Ghana meeting of the International Missionary Council (1957/8) for integration of that organisation into the World Council of Churches, and at Ghana the decision was taken to merge them.

M.A.C. Warren was the only member of the Committee to voice misgivings at the time, though he also eventually voted for integration. Warren was concerned that the merger would alienate Evangelicals. He was also, as a historian, convinced of the importance of the voluntarism which had produced and sustained the missionary societies (cf. Walls 1988). He was wary of centralization and bureaucracy which reduced spontaneity and flexibility in mission advocating instead "the independence of the mission" (Warren 1951; see also Yates 1994:138-143,155-157).

The decision of Ghana was effected at New Delhi in 1961 when the IMC became a division (later sub-unit) of the WCC[2] and the WCC amended its "Basis" to make it more missionary.[3] In the opening session, Lesslie Newbigin, then General Secretary of the IMC, welcomed integration as "a vital contribution to both the missionary life of the Church and to the ecumenical character of the Christian mission". He reminded the WCC of its origins in the missionary movement but, in a far-sighted comment, he warned

---

[2] Now the Commission of World Mission and Evangelism (CWME).

[3] The WCC was defined as "a fellowship of churches which *accept* the Lord Jesus Christ as God and Saviour" (in place of *confess*) and the words "and therefore seek to fulfil together their common calling to the glory of one God, Father, Son and Holy Spirit" were added.

of the danger of "a false use of the word 'ecumenical' which omits the missionary dimension" (WCC 1961:3-4).

Despite the apparent theological soundness of integration, in practice the new structure meant that the voice of the missionary societies was seldom heard in the WCC. Instead in 1966, as Warren had predicted they would, the Evangelical missionary societies came together in an unprecedented way at Berlin and Wheaton launching a worldwide Evangelical missionary movement distinct from the WCC. They believed that "contemporary Protestant movements" were blurring "the biblical distinction between church and mission" (*The Wheaton Declaration* in Hedlund 1993:171).

Historians of mission have traced a pattern of voluntarism in mission through all the ages of the church. Ralph D. Winter, for example, argues from biblical and historical considerations for a two-structure theory of mission. In the New Testament he notes how Paul's missionary band worked in partnership with the churches. Throughout history, he believes, God has used both modalities (the church) and sodalities (missionary bands) in his mission. The cause of mission is found to be best served when these achieved a "synthesis" as in medieval Catholicism. In such an arrangement, according to Winter, successive sodalities are the source of the revival of the missionary vision and vitality of the modality/church (Winter & Hawthorne 1981:178-190; cf. Walls 1988).

This reading of history bears out a deep-seated Evangelical conviction that the church will soon lose its missionary vision without a voluntary society or sodality to promote it. The Christian Institute for the Study of Religion and Society (CISRS) Biennial Consultation in 1970, considering church unity in the Indian context, also came to the conclusion that it may be necessary for the sake of mission to have "breakaway movements within the Church" which are committed to certain intermediary goals in society (CISRS 1970:90). Commenting on this, T.V. Philip deduces that "it is only by keeping both unity and mission in continuous tension within one fellowship that the Church can truly understand the nature of its unity and its mission" (Philip 1970:95). He

109

illustrates this with the example of the early Church. He sees the Jerusalem Council (Acts 15) as an attempt to re-interpret the meaning of unity in the light of the challenge of the contemporary missionary situation in which Gentiles were turning to Christ. (*ibid.*)

The missionary nature of the church does not demand that all missionary activity be subordinated to a church. The mission and church mutually critique each other. The tendencies of the church to become self-absorbed and cut off from the realities of society are rebuked by the prophetic role of the mission. The tendencies of the mission to independence, divisiveness and permanence are rebuked by presence and faithfulness of the church. The mission revives the church and the church moderates the mission. Thus the creative tension of mission and unity is safeguarded and fostered by a certain autonomy of the mission.

It can be said that a similar rule applies in the case of missiology and theology. Orlando Costas puts the case very well. Noting that "mission is the mother of theology", Costas argues that "missiology serves as catalyst in theological education in any given historical situation". He elaborates,

> Missiology brings into focus new questions for the theological agenda, it sharpens theology's call for universality, and helps theology recognize the contextual limitations of all religious thought... Missiology contends against all theological provincialism, advocating an intercultural perspective in theology. Missiology questions all theological discourse that does not seriously consider the missionary streams of the Christian faith; all biblical interpretation that ignores the missionary motives that shape biblical faith; all the history of Christianity that omits the expansion of Christianity across cultural, social, and religious frontiers; and all pastoral theology that does not take seriously the mandate to communicate the Gospel fully and to the heart of the concrete situations of daily life... Missiology also enriches theology because it puts theology in contact with the worldwide Church with all its cultural and theological diversity (1994:14-15).

The missionary nature of the church means that mission has an essential place in the life of the church. But the concern of God is with the world and the *missio Dei* can never be limited by any human institution.

3. Uppsala 1968: The Cosmic Christ and the Unity of Humankind

In addition to arguing for a distinction of church and mission, Evangelicals also emphasise the distinctiveness of the church *vis-a-vis* the world. They have a strong sense of Christian identity. Evangelicals are worried about losing the uniqueness of the church and her Lord in endeavours toward unity. They refuse to see the church as merely one of the agents in a cosmic process but believe that "The Church is at the very centre of God's cosmic purpose and is his appointed means of spreading the gospel" (*Lausanne Covenant*: para. 6).

As the Ecumenical Movement embraced a mission to bring about unity, for many Evangelicals they seemed to lose the traditional Christian distinctions between the Creator and the created. God and the world become the same thing and Jesus Christ and his Church as the intermediary become no longer necessary. They therefore reject any cosmic Christ christology which unites the world in a socio-political utopia or in pantheistic eco-system. Salvation, for Evangelicals, is a gift of God which human beings must explicitly accept or else refuse.

The emphasis on the distinction between Creator and created in Evangelical theology lies in its strong emphasis on the holiness of God and the sinfulness of human beings. Sin is understood as a personal capitulation to temptation which results in a deep chasm between God and human beings that is bridgeable only by Jesus Christ. The Christian mission is therefore understood primarily as calling individuals to repent of their sins and turn to Jesus Christ. Mission aims at conversion, meaning repentance and explicit confession of the name of Jesus Christ.

In the run-up to Uppsala 1968, Donald McGavran, laid a challenge before the WCC in the form of an article entitled, "Will Uppsala Betray the Two Billion?" (Hedlund 1993:235-241). The "two billion" refers to those "who either have never heard of Jesus Christ or have no real chance to believe in him as Lord and Saviour" (*ibid.* 235). He criticised the WCC's preoccupation with socio-political and ecological issues while ignoring the biblical mandate to evangelize. Reacting to the drafts for Section II "Renewal in Mission", McGavran noted that the draft said "nothing about the necessity of faith", "the two billion" or about "sending messengers". The chief thrust of the draft was not to reaching the unreached but to the renewal of existing churches. McGavran claimed this was "a totally new concept of mission" unrelated to "the experience and understanding of the universal church, the clear intent of the Bible, and the express statements of Jesus Christ our Lord". He saw the origins of this in the confusion of mission and ecumenism, "scarcely has mission appeared to be the business of the whole Church, than the Church has begun to subvert the mission to her own service" (*ibid.* 235-241). The protests of McGavran and others did result in some changes in the final document but did not substantially alter it.

In the continuing debate about the meaning of mission Evangelicals have reacted to movements for the unity of human-kind. Firstly, because the socio-political definitions of sin seemed to play down personal sinfulness (especially at the CWME meeting at Bangkok in 1973). And secondly because the unity of humankind blurred the identity of the church as the redeemed people of God. Many Evangelicals have also opposed inter-faith dialogue because it seems to rule out any call for conversion. Thus it appears to deny the uniqueness of Jesus Christ (cf. *Lausanne Covenant*: para. 3). Similarly the unity of creation appears to be a peripheral concern in the light of the lostness of the unevangelized and the imminent return of Christ.

While not denying the intention of God to unite all things in Christ, the goal of mission cannot be reduced to unity. God's sending activity also has other dimensions not easily accommodated under the heading of "unity".

Within the Ecumenical Movement itself there has been further reflection on what kind of unity is desirable. The Second World Conference on Faith and Order at Edinburgh in 1938 made corporate or organic union the highest form of unity (Crow 1987: 396). However recently organic unions have fallen out of favour partly because they do not take sufficient account of what could be described as the *missionary situation* of the church. That is, they do not sufficiently allow for diversity and they tend to minimise issues of justice and truth (Crow 1987; Deschner 1991).

Challenged by a pluralistic world and global inequalities, the ecumenical world has recognised that the goal of mission is "more than inclusiveness" (Deschner 1991:57-67). Recent attempts to redefine unity has resulted in new models, Crow identifies five ways of describing "the unity we seek" (1987:396-402). Valuable though these models are, the number of different models of unity suggests that ecumenical endeavour is overstretched as a comprehensive term for mission. And David Bosch's multifaceted paradigm further implies that ecumenical endeavour is only one way of looking at mission (Bosch 1991:368-510). T.V. Philip sums up the discussion from an Ecumenical perspective:

> What is clear in the present day discussion is that there is a dialectical tension between unity and mission and that this relationship should find theological and structural expression in a united church (1994:108).

A healthy Christian identity *vis-a-vis* the world results from the creative interaction of ecumenical endeavour and mission.

4. Canberra 1991: The Spirit and the Spirits

The theme of the Canberra Assembly was "Come Holy Spirit — Renew the Whole Creation", the first time the third Person of the Trinity had been the focus of a WCC Assembly. It followed in the wake of the Second Lausanne Congress in Manila (1989) which echoed some of the ecumenical concerns for the socio-political and ecological dimensions of mission. But the Evangelicals present at Canberra, led by Vinay Samuel, felt it necessary to add a statement of "Evangelical Perspectives From Canberra" (Kinnamon 1992:282-286/Ro & Nicholls 1993:38-43). This was generally positive and recognised many lessons that Evangelicals could learn from the Ecumenical Movement. But it sounded several cautionary notes, notably in the area of theology:

113

The ecumenical movement needs a theology rooted in the Christian revelation and relevant to contemporary problems. At present, there is insufficient clarity regarding the relationship between the confession of the Lord Jesus Christ and Saviour according to scripture, the person and work of the Holy Spirit, and legitimate concerns which are part of the WCC agenda (*ibid.* 283/39).[4]

In the Evangelical world generally the response to Canberra focused on the contribution of Chung Hyun Kyung which seemed to confirm Evangelical fears that the WCC was syncretistic. In *Beyond Canberra* (Ro & Nicholls, eds. 1993) a number of Evangelicals have responded. The editors lament the absence of any discussion of the work of the Holy Spirit in conversion and renewal of churches (*ibid.* 7). David Parker draws attention to the close association of the work of the Spirit with the work of the Son in Scripture and to the biblical emphasis on the fulness of the Spirit's presence in the church (*ibid.* 14). That the Spirit is the Spirit of holiness, purity, separation was also absent from the discussions.

Rene Padilla detects within the WCC a "growing dissatisfaction with the idea that... for the sake of unity no theological position must be rejected as heretical" (*ibid.* 31-34). Indeed, D. Preman Niles has posed the question, "How Ecumenical Must the Ecumenical Movement Be?" (Niles 1991: title). A dilemma which mirrors Stephen Neill's famous dictum, "If everything is mission, nothing is mission" (Neill 1959:81). A broadening of either unity or mission so that the one swallows up the other is to the detriment of both.

The rediscovery of the work of the Holy Spirit in the world to renew the whole creation is a welcome one but this needs to be balanced by the awareness of the special work of the Spirit in God's people who have been baptized by the Spirit. The Spirit is the Spirit of unity and ecumenical endeavour but the Spirit is also

---

[4] The Evangelical "Perspectives" were found to be very close to the Orthodox "Reflections" (in Kinnamon 1992: 279-282/Ro & Nicholls 1993: 49-52) and this has prompted further dialogue between these two groups.

the Spirit of mission. It is precisely because the Spirit is at work not only in the church but also in a different way in the world that mission must be distinct from ecumenical endeavour. The Holy Spirit of Pentecost moves freely and is not limited by the borders of the church, nor by unity or otherwise of believers. The work of the Spirit in the world and the work of the Spirit in the church should each be understood in view of the other.

V. Conclusion

Theologically speaking, mission and unity belong together because they are both attributes of God, they are both part of God's intention in Jesus Christ, and they are both the work of the Spirit. But they should not be confused. Mission and unity are only fully comprehended when they are distinguished and seen in the light of each other. Mission and ecumenical endeavour stand in a relationship of tension but this tension can be creatively utilised to bring about God's purposes.

References

Amirtham, Sam (1980) "The Quest for Church Unity in India" in *Ecumenism in India*, New Delhi: ISPCK.

Bosch, David J. (1991) *Transforming Mission: Paradigm Shifts in Theology of Mission*, Maryknoll, NY: Orbis.

Boer, Harry R. (1961) *Pentecost and Missions*, Grand Rapids, MI: Eerdmans.

Christian Institute for the Study of Religion and Society (1970) Biennial Consultation Findings, *Religion and Society*, Vol. XVII, No.1, March.

Costas, Orlando E. (1994) "Theological Education and Mission" in C. Rene Padilla (ed.), *New Alternatives in Theological Education*, Oxford: Regnum.

Crow Jr., Paul A. (1987) "Ecumenics as Reflections on Models of Christian Unity" in *Ecumenical Review*, Vol.39, pp.389-403.

Deschner, John (1991) "More Than Inclusiveness" in *Ecumenical Review*, Vol.43, pp.57-67.

Goodall, Norman (ed.) (1953) *Missions Under the Cross* (Willingen 1952), London: IMC.

Hedlund, Roger E. (1993) *Roots of the Great Debate in Mission: Mission in Historical and Theological Perspective*, Bangalore: Theological Book Trust.

Joint Working Group of the RCC and the WCC (1984) *Common Witness*, Geneva: WCC/Rome: SPCU.

Lausanne Committee for World Evangelization (1989), *The Manila Manifesto: An Elaboration of the Lausanne Covenant Fifteen Years Later*, Pasadena, CA: LCWE.

Mueller-Fahrenholz, Geiko (1978) *Unity in Today's World: The Faith and Order Studies on Unity of the Church-Unity of Humankind*, Geneva: WCC.

Neill, Stephen (1959) *Creative Tension: The Duff Lectures, 1958*, London: Edinburgh House.

Neill, Stephen (1960) *Men of Unity*, London: SCM.

Newbigin, Lesslie (1964[1953]) *The Household of God*, London: SCM.

Niles, D. Preman (1991) "How Evangelical Must the Ecumenical Movement Be?" in *Ecumenical Review*, Vol.43, No.4, pp.451-458.

Orchard, Ronald K. (1958) *The Ghana Assembly of the IMC*, London: Edinburgh House.

Philip, T.V. (1970) "The Nature of the Unity We Seek", in *NCC Review*, Vol.90, No.3, pp.92-96.

Philip, T.V. (1994) *Ecumenism in Asia*, Delhi: ISPCK.

Ro, Bong Rin & Bruce J. Nicholls (eds.) (1993) *Beyond Canberra: Evangelical Responses to Contemporary Ecumenical Issues*, Oxford: Regnum.

Rouse, Ruth & Stephen C. Neill (1993[1954]) *A History of the Ecumenical Movement 1517-1948*, Geneva: WCC.

Sadiq, J.W. (1976) "An Assessment of Church Unions in India", *Indian Journal of Theology*, Vol.25, pp.159-166.

Sundkler, Bengt (1965) *Church of South India: The Movement Towards Union, 1900-1947*, London: Lutterworth.

Taylor, John V. (1972) *The Go-Between God: The Holy Spirit and the Christian Mission*, London: SCM.

Walls, Andrew F. (1988) "Missionary Societies and the Fortunate

Subversion of the Church", *The Evangelical Quarterly*, Vol.88, pp.141-155.

Warren, M.A.C. (1951) *The Christian Mission*, London: SCM.

Winter, Ralph D. (1973) "The Two Structures of God's Redemptive Mission" in Ralph D. Winter and Steven C. Hawthorne (eds.), *Perspectives on the World Christian Movement*, Pasadena: William Carey Library.

World Council of Churches (1962) *The New Delhi Report*, London: SCM.

Yates, Timothy (1994) *Christian Mission in the Twentieth Century*, Cambridge: CUP.

CHAPTER 6

Popular Religions and Mission

Joseph Valiamangalam*

I. Introduction

The Synod of Bishops (1974) on Evangelization and *Evangelii Nuntiandi* (1975), the Apostolic Exhortation which followed, have both highlighted the need of rediscovering the value of popular religiosity by the Church in order to incarnate the gospel in a particular culture and to evangelize that culture. According to Pope Paul VI:

> What matters is to evangelize man's culture and cultures... Though independent of cultures the Gospel and evangelization are not necessarily incompatible with them... The split between the Gospel and culture is without doubt the drama of our time, just as it was of other times. Therefore every effort must be made to ensure a full evangelization of culture, or more correctly of cultures (EN 20).

I strongly believe that the Church and missiologists have to take seriously the phenomenon of popular culture and popular religiosity in our evangelizing action and reflection in order to evolve meaningful methods of evangelizing culture and make the Gospel meaningful to the people of India today.

This paper is an attempt to explore the missiological implications of popular religions in the context of the Church's evan-

* *Joseph Valiamangalam is on the staff of the Gujarat Jesuit Regional Theologate. He holds a licentiate in missiology from the Gregorian University, Rome. Presently he is pursuing doctoral studies in missiology.*

gelizing activity with particular reference to the popular religiosity of Gujarat.

II. Various Approaches to Popular Religions

1. Popular Religion and Higher Religions

The experience of being colonized has kindled the ideology of nationalism in the educated political and intellectual elites of India. At the same time Hindu politicians and religious leaders, particularly the Rastriya Swayam Sevak Sangh (RSS) and Bharatiya Janata Party (BJP) have been trying to define who is a true Indian. They see the conversion work of Christian missionaries of converting people to Christianity in India and the Islamisation of non-Muslims in Pakistan as a threat to Indian sovereignty, and so they define a true Indian as a true Hindu. It means if you are not a follower of Hinduism, you are not a true nationalist. They make all-out organized efforts through propaganda and even Government Reservation Policy to absorb into Hinduism the adivasis and tribals and the scheduled castes or dalits who were 'untouchable' and were kept out of Hindu society till the recent past (Valiamangalam 1996:139).

At the same time there is a growing political consciousness of the need to define their religious and political identity among marginalised people, religious minorities and dalits who are trying to maintain their autonomy in political as well as religious and cultural life and who refuse to accept the dominant ideology of 'Hindutva'.

2. Anthropological View of Popular Religions

Anthropologists have abandoned the classical view of culture in which the elite who are educated, intelligent and powerful are the only ones who are cultured and they control not only politics and economics but also religion, through monopolizing the religious institutions, interpreting scriptures and regulating the cult and the rituals.

In this view the people are considered as mass: ignorant, immature, moved by sentiments and superstitions rather than reason. Popular religion is the religion of the ignorant people, who are incapable of having mature adult faith and are moved by sentiments and superstitions.

The romantic view of culture sees in the people creativity and originality, freshness of intuition, sentiments and a profound sense of God. All these will be missing in the dominant, rationally cold elite who are more interested essentially in conserving and improving their power over the people, especially with the support of the official religious institutions to which they are affiliated.

In the above description, popular religion is the expression of popular religious sentiments as opposed to the official religion which is supported by the dominant class. So it is clear that the term popular religion is not neutral, but is loaded with value judgement according to one's concept of religion and of people.

The privileged upper-class elite in society usually determine the way of understanding a society. They are supposed to be the locus of interpretation, meaning and value of society in the classical understanding. Can social meaning be gained from the lower levels of the social structure? The field work of anthropologists like Robert Redfield and Clifford Geertz have set forth the notion that a positive and necessary notion of knowledge of society could be gained from its lower levels so that this strata is seen as the locus of interpretation, meaning and value. It means that the positive meaning of a society is represented by the common people, the folk. Robert Redfield distinguishes these two understandings: the elite religion and culture he describes as the Great Tradition and the folk religion and culture is described as the Little Tradition.

3. Marxist View of Popular Religion According to Marx:

Religious distress is at the same time the expression of real distress and the protest against real distress. Religion is the sigh of the oppressed creature, the heart of a heartless world, just as it is the spirit of the spiritless situation. It is the opium of the people.[1]

---

[1] Karl Marx, "*Introduction to a Critique of Hegel's Philosophy of Right*" (1844) quoted by Harvey Cox in *The Seduction of the Spirit*, New York, 1973, p.115.

According to Marxist analysis, the dominating oppressors want to maintain the status quo and so they force the oppressed to imbibe the dominant cultural values and be submissive. The oppressed at the same time need to be conscious of their oppression and desire to get involved for the revolutionary transformation of society. For Marxists popular religion is thus the religion of the subaltern class.

4. The Church's Approach to Popular Religion

Christian missionaries have been accused of trying to civilize the natives as part of their missionary activity. As children of their age, it was but natural that they tacitly approved of the classical theory of culture in which European culture was considered superior and the culture of the native people was either inferior or 'primitive'. At the same time the missionaries were pioneers in the empirical study of culture which paved the way for modern Anthropology which has proved that no culture is superior or inferior in comparison to any other culture.

The history of mission in India shows that Francis Xavier did not get sufficient exposure to the religious traditions of India, while Beschi and De Nobili and others like them really got to know Hinduism in depth by studying Vedic literature and Hindu philosophy. They also interacted with high caste Brahmins in order to win them over to Christianity with limited success. The Hindu elite like Raja Ram Mohun Roy who came into contact with Christianity through Western education was challenged by the Christian philosophy of equality and justice and service to the poor. They were not much appreciative of the conversion work of missionaries. At the same time contact with Christianity and Western culture made the Hindu elite wake up from religious stagnation, revive Hinduism and take up nationalism.

Thus there was a process of mutual give-and-take between the Hindu elite and the Christianity preached and lived by the colonizers and missionaries. Because of the experience of coming into contact with Christianity through the colonizers and European missionaries who are seen as agents of the colonizers by the Hindu elite, Christian missionaries could not make much headway in evangelization with them, except running prestigious schools and other educational institutions for their benefit.

Christian missionaries were more successful among the tribals especially in Chotanagpur and in the North East. Here the missionaries were able to study and appreciate the tribals' culture and religious practices and adapt and inculturate them successfully. They were able to educate the tribals and free them from the clutches of money lenders and help them to regain their self dignity and self-identity as Tribals. They were also able to develop their own tribal theology which shows that Christianity has taken deep roots among them.

Mass conversions to Christianity took place among the dalits in most states in India during the colonial period. The missionaries appeared as saviours to the socially and religiously oppressed and marginalised dalits who were denied education and entry into temples by the caste Hindus. The schools, hospitals and other welfare programmes started by the missionaries helped the dalits to become Christians and get out of the centuries-old curse of caste discrimination and thus gain some self respect. The missionaries were either not well equipped to appreciate the popular culture of the oppressed or they were so overwhelmed by the problems they faced in evangelizing the dalits that they could not find sufficient time and other resources to study deeper their culture and religion. Due to the 'sanskritization' process the educated dalits in general were ashamed of their culture and would try to adopt the religion of the dominant high caste Hinduism. Ambedkar tried to conscientize the dalits by taking them to Buddhism and also organizing them politically. Now attempts are made by the Christian dalits to evolve a dalit theology.

As mentioned above, *Evangelii Nuntiandi* urges the local churches to 'discover the people' and their culture and religion as a valid approach to the interpretation of culture in order to evangelize culture. The Church in India and especially missiologists are being challenged today not only to dialogue with the Hinduism and Buddhism of the Great Tradition[2] but to enter into a deeper

---

[2] See *Arun Shourie and His Christian Critic*, Voice of India, New Delhi, 1995, an example of dialogue between Augustine Kanjamala and Arun Shourie.

participation in the life, struggles and culture of the majority of the people who belong to the Little Tradition.

III. Definition of Popular Religion

For Harvey Cox (1974:14),

Popular religion is that cluster of memories and myths, hopes and images, rites and customs that pulls together the life of a person or group into a meaningful whole. It lends coherence to life, furnishes a fund of meanings, gives unity to human events and guides people in making decisions.

Robert Towler defines popular religion as

those beliefs and practices of an overtly religious nature which are not under domination of a prevailing religious institution[3]

Popular religion is attractive to the masses because they are spontaneous and agreeable to their manner of thinking and feeling and it satisfies the inner urge to piety. It has a spontaneous and festive character. By naming popular, it can be understood as anything which springs from 'the people' and is distinguished from that which is institutional and official (Arulsamy 1986:58).

Paul VI in *Evangelii Nuntiandi* says that

Popular religiosity is rich in values. It manifests a t h i r s t for God which only the simple and poor can know. Popular religiosity manifests itself as seeking the meaning of life. It is a cry of hope of the people who desire to live a life together in fraternity and equality. Popular religiosity is a search for security and salvation (n 48).

1. Characteristics of Popular Religion

Among the several characteristics of popular religion (Galilea 1987:441) the following may be noted:

First, there is a tendency toward freedom and autonomy in which the simple people find emotional support. For example, in

---

[3] Quoted by Felix Wilfred in Paul Puthanangady, (ed.) *Popular Devotions*, p.594.

Christianity, though popular religiosity uses religious channels to express itself, it emphasizes values and practices that do not always follow official teaching. Hence, the feasts of saints and that of Mother Mary may be more important than those of Christ.

Second, it stresses devotions and religious symbols as mediations of God. It celebrates the presence of God in nature, in images and in special places considered holy. As heart and sentiments are stressed in popular religion, relationship to God is expressed through narratives, images, places, things and persons which speak directly to the heart.

Third, it manifests a strong sense of God's presence in everyday life. God is seen as intervening continuously in favour of His children and this intervention can be in response to the promises of the people to undertake some penance or vows to be fulfilled if the favour is granted.

Fourth, popular religiosity is the vehicle for communicating the experience of God. Processions and pilgrimages to shrines and holy places on foot is believed to bestow special graces and experience of God which for most religious minded rural folk may be the climax of their religious experience during the year.

Fifth, popular religion is strongly linked to the rites of passage which are crucial stages of human life. Through the rites and rituals of birth, puberty, marriage and death, people find the presence and protection of God.

Sixth, it upholds the religious values of the ordinary people and the weak who are ignored by the elite who hold power and who make decisions in society. Popular religion makes us aware that our attitude towards the needy had to do with God and with goodness and evil in human life. So popular religiosity is based not only on ritual expressions but also on the experience of solidarity and compassion among the ordinary, poor people in society.

2. Popular Religion, Folklore, Superstition and Magic

Folklore is the sum total of beliefs, rites and ceremonies, legends, myths, festivals, fears and superstitions which are common to a certain cultural area. The cycle of life (Michael 1990)

— birth, betrothal, marriage, death — and the annual cycle of seasons, of family, work and social life are all filled with beliefs, rituals, feasts and festivals (James 1961). People need to eliminate the fear of malign spirits and implore the help of benevolent spirits.

Superstition means literally "to put above". Often people seek protection and security in superstitious practices due to the insecurities of life. They use tangible things like medals, amulets and charms to seek divine help, protection and favours. Superstitions diminish people's sense of responsibility for their life, their actions and their future (Saldanha 1986:46).

3. Popular Religion and Pilgrimages

Pilgrimages are a common element in all the popular religions (Turner 1974:167-230). Certain places are perceived by the people as holy and identified by them as having a special relationship with the life of faith of a people, inspiring them in their faith, hope, commitment and surrender to God in many ways. The places can be mountains or the places of birth of founders of religions or sects or rivers or forests or temples.

Usually pilgrims fast while making the journey on foot as external form of penance, to purify themselves. Purity of mind is considered the greatest of all pilgrimages. High moral and spiritual qualities are to be cultivated to obtain the full reward of pilgrimages. The climax of the journey can be making an offering or darshan of the deity, or making confession, hearing holy mass, receiving holy communion and taking home prasad or a sacred picture (Amaladoss 1986:71).

Pilgrimages strengthen the life of faith of a people and serve as a vehicle of their communion with the divine. They help the people to interpret their life and enable them to face the problems of life with renewed strength.

IV. Popular Religiosity in Gujarat

Now let us study some of the features of popular religiosity currently being practised in Gujarat.

The ordinary people belonging to different tribes and castes are faced with insecurity, sickness and misfortune in their daily life. In order to face these insecurities and also to keep morality as social control, they take recourse to different gods according to their particular needs. Thus when the maximum number of children used to die due to smallpox, *Sitalamata* was accepted as the goddess of smallpox. In the case of sterility, *Meldi Mata* is invoked to obtain children. The shepherds who move around the fields have recourse to the snake god *Goghabapa*.

Since systematic philosophical thought and logic are not developed among the tribes and lower castes, they turn to superstitious practices. The *bhuvo* or medicine man plays an important role in their life. He would offer the sacrificial goat to the gods since gods are believed to be pleased with sacrifices. Sometimes they even resort to child sacrifice to obtain certain favours from gods (Times of India 1996:1).

Among the lower caste people certain festivals and celebrations play an important part in their religiosity. They celebrate *divaso* to remember their ancestors. Holi is considered the festival of shudras. However, people would normally say "we enjoy this", "we feel at home and it is our celebration".

At the entrance to the villages in Gujarat there are carved stone monuments which are called *paliyas*. These are erected to revere the martyred heroes who have sacrificed their lives to defend the honour of women, or to protect the cows or the village from dacoits. People identify themselves with the heroism of the village martyrs and heroes.

Worship of goddess *Shakti* is the most wide spread form of worship in popular religion in Gujarat. Mythology says that when Lord Shiva carried Parvati in the sky, her limbs fell at sixty-four different places, among which are Pavagadh, Ambaji and Bahucharaji in Gujarat. Ambaji is the most popular pilgrim centre in Gujarat. People take the first born child to shave his head there and seek the blessings of *Amba Mataji*. Vishnu is worshipped in Somnath which is supposed to have one of the twelve *jyotirlingas* in the country.

Popular religiosity in Gujarat is highly influenced by Jainism and also by *Sankaracharya*. People's religiosity is also nourished by wandering saints and gurus who give religious discourses. In their discourses they stress less on philosophy but highlight more on morality that suits the community and the audience. The Saurashtra region in Gujarat is known as the land of *jati-satis*, that is the land of holy men and *satis* or women who have followed their dead husbands to the funeral pyre. Harijan saints like Gangabai, Jivan Sati, Bhakta Giga and others through their bhajans support the devotional life of ordinary people. Gandhiji tried to purify the popular religiosity of his time when he popularized the eleven vows which were already in vogue among the populace irrespective of caste. The saints exhorted the people to observe humbly and firmly the following eleven great vows:

Truth, non-violence, not to steal, not to store what is not needed, *brahmacharya* and self-effort, removal of untouchability, hospitality, *swadeshi*, renunciation of tasty food, and equal respect for all religions.

What I have described above is the spontaneous religious world of the ordinary people of different castes in the villages and towns of Gujarat. The picture emerging from the above description is very different from the stereotype images and descriptions which people are made to believe of high Hinduism based on the Vedas and Upanishads and the Samskaras and which are highly ritualistic and controlled by the elite and the priestly hierarchy.

V. *Missiological Perspectives on Popular Religion*

Theological developments in Latin American countries like Brazil, Argentina, Colombia etc. and African countries like Zaire point to the emerging trend in the evangelizing activity of the Church where the popular culture of the poor, the humble and the powerless people, is emerging as the point of reference. Missiological tools for reflection and action in evangelization therefore, have to take up the challenge proposed by Vatican II in its Decree *Ad Gentes:*

If this goal is to be achieved, theological investigation must necessarily be stirred up in each major socio-cultural area.

Thus it will be more clearly seen in what ways faith can seek for understanding in the philosophy and wisdom of these people (AG 22).

The Church in India need to take this challenge seriously and discern how to get involved in the experience of people who follow popular religions and who form the majority of the people of India. We derive our motivation for this from the mystery of Christ: the incarnation, *kenosis* and the mission entrusted by Christ to the Church.

1. The Incarnation, Kenosis and Mission

The dynamics of the incarnation show that though Jesus was born into the Jewish culture and became part of it, he was not possessed by Jewish culture alone and his message is not monopolized by any one particular culture. Jesus and his message cannot be identified with any one culture. He can incarnate in the Jewish or Greek-Latin culture as well as in Asian and African cultures: not only in elite cultures but also in the popular cultures of the poor, humble and powerless which include their religiosity as well.

Jesus the Wisdom of God empties himself and makes himself understood not by the wise and prudent elites of this world, but by the poor and humble who are rejected and exploited by the wise elite of the world. The religiosity and culture of the ordinary people possess the living wisdom which nourishes the people and gives them an experience of God's revelation to them in their existential situation of powerlessness, sickness and many other negative experiences of life.

Jesus is sent to all humankind and his mission is universal. Yet the poor were and are his special concern. The Church also is sent to all peoples, but in a privileged way to the most marginalised. It is a sign of the authenticity of the Church's mission, as pointed out aptly by Pope Paul VI in *Evangelii Nuntiandi:*

And among all these signs there is the one to which he attaches great importance: the humble and the poor are evangelized, become his disciples and gather together "in his

129

name", in the great community of those who believe in him (EN 12).

Now let us see the implications of this understanding in the various spheres of the evangelizing activity of the Church today.

2. Popular Religion and Dialogue

As we have seen above, popular religiosity reflects the actual God-experience of the vast majority of the people. It is evident that it is the popular religions that represent the reality of the religious experience of most of the people. The mission of dialogue of the Church in actual practice, therefore, should not be so much a dialogue with the institutionalized religions of the 'Great Tradition' but with the people's religion of the 'Little Tradition' in their concrete daily life. Theological reflection and statements of Church authorities in general seem to show preference for dialogue with the institutionalized religions which possess developed philosophies and have intellectuals and priests who expound the doctrines of these religions.

Zeitler (1986:112) points out the marvellous example of Buddhism in Japan which entered into dialogue with the popular Japanese religions and succeeded in becoming a Japanese religion whereas Christianity was not successful. Whenever Buddhism entered a new area it presented itself as a supplement to the existing religions and not as their rival. In this way Buddhism has reached the local cultures and religions and adjusted itself to the genius of the various peoples and cultures of Asia without destroying them.

3. Popular Religion and Inculturation

Popular religion is part of the cultural heritage of a people which is to be maintained and promoted according to Vatican II (NA 2). It is like flowers that grow spontaneously in such great and amazing variety in the jungles that surround our cultivated gardens. It is the same life, and there would be no garden if there were not first the free, exuberant growth of life in the forests (Neuner 1986:32). When the prevailing trend is for the dominant culture to absorb all sub-cultures, it is the duty of the evangelizing mission of the Church to help people preserve their identity and spontaneity without any manipulation of their culture.

Though the Churches have been involved in the lives of ordinary poor and marginalised people through education, health work and developmental activities, it may be said that their religious life and culture were not touched by our activities. By and large we have not taken the myths, symbols, legends and celebrations of the people seriously to accept them as vehicles of God's revelation to them and as agents of God experience for the people.

Genuine inculturation demands that we shed the condescending attitude in our efforts to relate to the people and their religion. Also we need to abandon the attitude of 'studying' their culture and religion as does a university scholar. We need to shed the role of the investigator and become seekers like the anthropologist Carlos Castaneda (Castaneda 1971) as he himself describes how he became an apprentice to learn from the inside.

4. Popular Religion and Liberation

The tendency of organized religions is to control and absorb the popular religiosity of the people. Today in the name of cultural nationalism the Sangh Parivar is using popular religion to disseminate Hindu identity (Michael 1986:185-197), for example their organizing in a mass scale *Janmastami, Navratri, Ganesh Chaturthi, Raksha bandhan* and pilgrimages. The elite in these religions look at the popular religious experience of the ordinary, marginalized people with condescension and fail to appreciate the rich potential of popular religions to lead the people to self-respect and freedom. The Marxists and other social activists, including the Christian social activists, depend to a great extent on the Marxist analysis of society and often fail to take popular culture and religiosity seriously. They fail to see or refuse to accept that popular religious symbols have given the powerless poor and oppressed their identity and have given them strength to resist and free themselves from social, economic and political oppression. On the other hand, there is the natural tendency as we have seen earlier for popular religion to maintain the status quo and become reactionary in its attitude to change. It is most vulnerable to the risks of superstitions and magic due to the utilitarian view of faith with a distorted idea of God; and it can be manipulated for one's selfish ends. Such devotions and distorted practices keep people engaged in their selfish pursuits, preventing the use of their energies for social change and revolt against oppressive structures.

Popular religiosity in the form of sects which are growing at a rapid pace is a sign that the marginalized people whose voice is not heard in the organized religions and who are treated as mere objects are asserting their identity and independence in their search for an experience of community. This can be a sign of protest against the elite religions.

Another positive sign in the marginalized and oppressed in India is the dalits who are getting organized and have begun the process of conscientising themselves and also critically evaluating themselves and their religion. This process should lead them to a liberating experience from all that has been alienating them from their genuine cultural self identity. This emerging consciousness should transform them from merely being objects of history to its subjects who know how to live in community where there is mutual respect and harmony with nature.

The Christian experience of Exodus and Easter can help the process of liberation in popular religions. The Exodus stands for the liberation of people from political and economic bondage. In Easter, which is the resurrection of Christ, the Church celebrates the liberation of all men and women from sin and death. It suggests that not even death can negate the significance of human life. Exodus-Easter experience shows us that God is that power which despite all setback never admits final defeat. God desires, inspires and supports all oppressed and marginalized people in their struggle for liberation from all forms of bondage (Cox 1974:152). The evangelising action of the Church can help popular religions to go through the process of Exodus-Easter, that is, the experience of death to all that keep them enslaved and of the resurrection to a new life in freedom.

VI. Conclusion

The Church is in a privileged time today when she is called by Christ through her evangelizing activity to get involved in the lives of ordinary, exploited and marginalized people. It means to enter into dialogue with the people's culture and religions and help them to liberate themselves from every form of falsehood, superstitions and magic. As evangelization is liberative of popular culture, the Church is also called to enter into the world views, symbols, myths and the deeper feelings of the marginalised and oppressed people. We need to be exposed to the faith of the ordinary people and as we identify ourselves to liberate and transform them, we in turn also should be open to share in the God experience, in the festivals, celebrations, devotions and pilgrimages which would liberate us to identify ourselves with the cause of the people. This means that the Church is challenged as evangelizer to enter into a serious, deep and sympathetic study of popular religions.

References

Amaladass, A. (1986) "Theology and Popular Devotions" in Paul Puthanangady, (ed.) *Popular Devotions*, Bangalore: N.B.C.L.C.

Arulsamy, S. (1986) "Popular Devotions an Experience of the Divine", in Paul Puthanangady, (ed.) *Popular Devotions*, Bangalore: N.B.C.L.C.

Castaneda, C. (1973) *A Separate Reality*, New York: Simon and Schuster.

Cox, H. (1973) *The Seduction of the Spirit*, New York: Simon and Schuster.

Galilea, S. (1987) "Popular Christian Religiosity" in Mircea Eliade (Ed.) *The Encyclopedia of Religion*, New York.

James, E. O. (1961) *Seasonal Feasts and Festivals*, London: Thames and Hudson.

Michael, S. M. (1986) "The politicization of the Ganapati Festival" in *Social Compass*, XXXIII/2-3, pp.185-197.

Michael, S. M. (1990) "Cultural Performance as Christian Celebrations" in *Indian Missiological Review*, April Vol.1.pp.76-90.

Neuner, J. (1986) "Popular Devotions: Theological Reflections", in Paul Puthanangady, (ed.) *Popular Devotions*, Bangalore: N.B.C.L.C.

Saldanha, J. (1986) "Popular Religiosity and Faith" in Paul Puthanangady, (ed.) *Popular Devotions*, Bangalore: N.B.C.L.C.

Times of India (1996) "Infants sacrificed to beget child", Ahmedabad, November 5.

Turner, V. (1974) "Pilgrimages as Social Process" in *Dramas, Fields and Metaphors*, Ithaca: New York.

Valiamangalam, J. (1996) "Conversion in Indian Religions" in J. Mattam and S. Kim (eds.), *Mission and Conversion: A Reappraisal*, Mumbai: St Pauls.

Zeitler, E. (1986) "Popular Christian Piety and Colonial Mission", in Paul Puthanangady, (ed.) *Popular Devotions*, Bangalore: N.B.C.L.C.

CHAPTER 7

Laity and Mission

J. Patmury*

I. Introduction

There is a great deal of talk in church circles at the present time about the importance of the laity. But, as J.H. Oldham, the founder of the Christian Frontier Council wrote more than four decades ago: The question is approached almost invariably from the wrong end. What is usually meant is that more laymen should come in and give their support to the Church as it is. That is just what a large number of the best lay people, at present standing on the fringe, will not do (1953:89).

In the church the assumption is, as Gibbs and Morton put it, that a lay person is one of the privates in God's army; and the officers are the clergy. The latter have the job of running the church, of deciding the doctrine, administering the sacraments and preaching in the church (1964:9). The laity are supposed to listen to them, receive the sacraments and be submissive.

If we ask a lawyer or a politician who a layman is, he would say: Someone who has not been trained in law or politics, someone who is an amateur, who does not understand, who is not an expert. This is, in fact the concept of the laity in the church. This concept is derived from the Middle Ages when education came to be accepted as the prerogative of the clergy, like the Brahmins of ancient India.

---

* J. Patmury has a doctorate in missiology and is at present Librarian and Associate Professor at UTC, Bangalore.

After the Barbarian invasions, there was a general lowering of culture and the disappearance of schools in the West. Learning became a sort of monopoly of the clergy and the monks, and from the late Middle Ages down to the Renaissance, literatus was synonymous with 'cleric' whereas the synonym for the "layman" was *illiteratus* or *idiotus* meaning a simple person, one who cannot explain things (Congar 1967:243). When this happened, the layman was indeed in an inferior position, outside the real life of the church, because of his ignorance. Then all who could read and write were regarded as clerical and those who could not were the laymen. The distinction was based not on the fact of ordination, but on the ability to read and write. The princes were practically the only laymen who had any say in the service of the church.

However the original meaning of the term laity did not have this negative connotation as we shall see presently.

II. The Meaning of Laity

The term laity in Christian theological circles today, refers to those members of the church who do not have the responsibilities of priestly functions appropriate to the office of the clergy or ordained ministers (Lusby 1989:425). This distinction was a later development which did not exist in the beginning of Christianity.

The term is derived from the Greek word *laikos* meaning "of or from the people". In early Christianity the term is derived from *laos* denoting "the chosen people of God", which is intimately connected with the term *ekklesia* (a called out people). From a Greco-Roman perspective *ekklesia* refers to official assemblies of voting citizens called to debate issues, select leaders and make decisions. The leaders and administrators chosen by them were subject to the community's review, praise and discipline (Wagner 1994:16).

In the New Testament, a layman is not a secular man, as is usually conceived today. The word, as mentioned above, is derived from *laos* which is used in the Bible to denote the people of God. The other peoples were the *ethne, nationes, gentes.*

136

III. Place of Laity in the Early Christian Communities

In the *ekklesia* of the first century Christianity the *laikos* had an important role though the term was never in vogue at that time. The church in those days resembled more closely the original vision of its founder. It was more egalitarian, in which the sharp distinction of hierarchy that was to be found later was non existent. Both men and women played important roles in the organisation, development and especially in the missionary task of the church. In the face of fierce persecution, Christianity made headway, even in the heart of the Roman empire, mainly due to the efforts of countless unknown ordinary men and women, mostly poor, unlettered slaves and housemaids.

Laymen and laywomen had a very important place especially in the Pauline house churches. Among the prominent persons mentioned in the Acts and Paul's letters we note: Aquila and Priscilla, a Jewish couple expelled from Rome by the edict of the emperor Claudius; they were of the same faith and occupation as Paul and were among the most trusted of his co-workers in Corinth. Titus was Paul's partner and fellow worker throughout his extended ministry in Ephesus. Crispus was the ruler of the synagogue in Corinth who was baptised by Paul himself. Cornelius was a Roman centurion stationed in Caesarea who was accepted into the community by Peter. Lydia, a travelling merchant who sold luxurious purple-dyed cloth for a living is remembered for her extended hospitality to Paul, Silas and the Christian community of Philippi. Stephanas, Paul's first convert in Corinth was strongly commended by Paul as one worthy of exercising authority in the church (1 Cor 16:15f). Fortunatus and Achaicus who brought information to Paul in Ephesus about the troubles in Corinth (1 Cor 16:17) were associates of Paul. Erastus, the city treasurer too was Paul's fellow worker.

Phoebe was a leading woman of the church in Cenchreae, commended by Paul in Romans 16:1-2 as worthy of special hospitality. Recommending her as she moved from Cenchreae, perhaps to Ephesus, Paul says: "I ask you to receive her in the Lord

137

in a way worthy of the saints and to give her any help she may need from you, for she herself has been *patron* (*prostatis*) of many and of me myself" (Rom 16:2). Most translations render the word *prostatis* as helper. James Dunn commending on this tendency remarks that the unwillingness of commentators to give prostatis its most natural and obvious sense of "*patron*" is very striking (Dunn 1986:888). The word, he says actually means "*patron*, protector" (or alternately, leader, ruler). The Latin equivalent *patronus* would be familiar to Paul's readers in reference to patronage of *collegia* or clubs. Phoebe was a lady of some stature who had acted as patron or protector for many, including Paul. She had business in Rome, quite probably a lawsuit. Whatever the business, Phoebe like Priscilla and Aquila and others could provide a variety of help for mission enterprise. The verses therefore contain a glimpse of the important role played by women in the early church (Dunn 1986:889). It is clear that in the early church, in the absence of strict hierarchical distinctions, and in an atmosphere of egalitarian structural setting every one felt he or she was directly responsible for the spread of the Gospel.

IV. Rise of the Clergy and the Formation of Hierarchy

However, before the end of the second century already the term *laikos* took on a more hierarchical connotation. Clement of Alexandria (c. 200 AD) uses the term to distinguish a layman from a deacon or a presbyter. By the third century we notice that the laity are assigned to the bottommost part of the ecclesiastical hierarchy. In the Didascalia Apostolorum, a third century Christian document, we read an instruction regarding the order of seating in the Christian assembly.

> For the priests, reserve a place in the eastern part of the house, and set the bishop's throne in the midst of them. The priests are to sit with him. Laymen are to take their place in the remainder of the eastern side of the house. It is fitting that the priests be placed in the eastern part of the house with the bishop, then the laymen, then the women. In this way, when

you rise to pray, the leaders will be able to rise first, then the laymen and then the women. If anyone finds himself in a place other than his own, the deacon who is inside is to take him, make him get up and lead him to the place which belongs to him... (Deiss 1967:88f).

V. Women at the very Bottom of the Hierarchy

We find here women at the very bottom of the hierarchy which was quite different at the beginning of Christianity. Luke reports that Jesus and his twelve chosen men were accompanied by a number of women. Named women went with Jesus to his death and burial. Such loyalty was a response to his unconventionality in holding religious discussion with women — even with a Samaritan woman.

This recognition continued even after the death of Jesus. The fourth Gospel tells us that Mary of Magdala was the first to see Jesus after the resurrection. In the Acts and the Letters of Paul as we saw above, we meet prominent women disciples such as Tabita, Lydia, Priscilla, Phoebe and others.

Gradually, as the Christian community develops ecclesiastically, the *kleros*, the leaders or those with 'office' become the ones through whom the means of grace are extended to the people, the *laikos*. By the time of the Council of Nicaea (325), the organisation and structure of the church was understood basically in terms of the clerical order with authority vested in the bishops and the Council as distinguished from the laity.

VI. Distinction Between the Clergy and the Laity

The distinction between the laity and the clergy in the Catholic tradition becomes correlative with a distinction between the church and the world. The clergy is believed to be ordained to the sacred order, with the right and responsibility of administering the Sacraments. The laity who are to receive the sacraments, and obey the teaching are to pursue their work in the world, the profane realm.

In the Eastern Orthodox Church a similar distinction is made

139

between the clergy and the laity. The most sacred area of the sanctuary behind the iconostasis, is inaccessible to lay persons during the Divine Liturgy and can be entered only by the priest.

Edward Schillebeeckx in two of his significant works: *Ministry* and *The Church with a Human Face* shows how the laity who had an equal place in the primitive Christian communities have progressively been degraded due to the increasing clericalization of the church in subsequent centuries.

In the earliest periods it was customary for both men and women to take the place of leadership in the churches that were founded by the apostles. It was natural that when these missionary apostles moved on, their functions of leadership and coordination should be taken over by obvious and spontaneous leaders in the various communities often the first converts and the first fellow workers, male or female... (Schillebeeckx 1982:8).

But soon the laity would lose their leadership and their right to preach in the church. Two significant events paved the way for the increasing clericalization of the church, namely, 1) the move away from house churches to the dedicated churches and 2) the imperial patronage of the clergy after the conversion of Constantine.

VII. From Dining Rooms to Assembly Halls

The literary and archaeological evidence of the second and third centuries point to the continued development of the churches away from the private household toward more elaborately established city-wide churches (Branick 1989:129). The movement away from the house churches would entail a loss particularly of the familial tone of the earliest Christian assemblies and the significant roles ordinary men and women played in them.

The image of the church as it emerges from the Acts of the Apostles and the Epistles, especially that of Paul, is one of a family. Christianity was conspicuous, and to many Pagans incomprehensible, as a religion without a temple. Luke describes house meetings as precisely the activity distinguishing the earliest Jerusalem believers from non-Christians (Acts 2:46; 5:42). The Christian home appears here as the exact counterpart to the Jewish temple. For Christians private homes afforded a place of privacy, intimacy and stability and Paul wrote of the assembly of the people as the temple of God. Paul lived and cultivated this family relationship with his co-workers and communities. Everyone felt that the church belonged to him or her and everyone felt the responsibility for the growth of the church.

The authority of the church as experienced in those house settings was brotherly-sisterly, fatherly-motherly type, an authority based on love and service as proposed by Christ. Christ had, in effect offended the clergy of his time when he challenged them: "Destroy this temple made of human hands". His message of the Kingdom in many ways was acultic (Branick 1989:135). God's loving presence was to be found in the lilies of the field and the birds of the air. Love and forgiveness took priority over prayer. The foundation of his church was built on slow witted fishermen and not on a high priest. The house settings reflected more closely the ideal set by Christ.

The movement away from the houses to more elaborately established churches will be accompanied by major shifts in the theology of the church. From roughly AD 150 we begin to notice adaptations and dedications of private residences for the exclusive use of worship. Along with this we notice a more significant change in the Lord's Supper itself. Once the bread and wine ritual was separated from a meal to become "the Eucharist", the community was no longer in a domestic setting (Branick 1989:133). The community now moves from the dining room to the assembly hall.

The development of the stylised meal seen as cultic ritual entailed a special shift in the role of the presider. He became the cultic leader, one who mediated God to the assembly. As the Eucharist was recognised as a sacrifice, the leader was seen as priest. A clergy developed, or more precisely, as Branick puts it, "a laity developed" (1989:133). Formal patterns of assembly and formal seating arrangements arose.

VIII. The Demise of the House Churches

At a meeting held sometime between AD 360 and 370, a synod of Laodicea forbade the holding of Eucharist in the home. The prohibition of Laodicea completes a critical cycle. It marked several changes. The Lord's Supper had changed from evening meal to a stylised ritual. The assembly had moved from the dining room to the sacred hall. Leadership shifted from family members to special clergy. Now *the original form of the church was declared illegal.* Branick notes:

> The cycle from house church to basilica epitomises the dialectic between original vision and later adaptation, between Scripture and Tradition. Jesus in the gospels chose people of various trades for leadership roles. He gathered the crowds in hill sides and lake shores. The later Christians needed a priestly caste of leaders conducting cult in sanctuaries. Paul wrote of the assembly of people as the temple of God; the later Christians understood the temple as a building (1989:134).

For about a century the private Christian dwelling had shaped the Christians' community life, forming the environment in which the Christians related to one another, providing an economic substructure, a platform for missionary work, a framework for leadership and authority and a definite role for laymen and laywomen.

The second century Christians seemed to have longed for a sacred space, a spot where God's presence could be enclosed. They appear to have longed for the sacred institution of the Old Testament.

IX. Laity Lose Their Right to Preach in the Church

In spite of the clericalization of the church by the time of the Council of Nicaea (325), the laity still had the power to preach in the church. But even this would come to an end during the Pontificate of Gregory IX. Commenting on this Schillebeeckx remarks:

> Gregory IX (1227-1241), by his prohibition of lay preaching, had seen preaching as the exclusive prerogative of the *ordo clericorum.* Up to the present day, there are still bish-

ops who claim that proclamation by a priest is qualitatively different from lay preaching. I find it a riddle to know on what mysterious factor such an assertion could be based (1985:188).

The clergy-laity relationship becomes one of shepherd and sheep. By this it is assumed that the clergy have the responsibility of leading the laity and the latter have the duty of following the clergy. Gregory of Nazianzus said: "Sheep, do not tend your shepherds, do not judge your judges, do not make laws for your lawmakers" and Pope Celestine said: "The people must be taught, not followed" (Congar 1967:241).

Alphonso Aguirre commenting on the imagery of the sheep and shepherd, brings to our notice that in real life it is the shepherd who is quite literally led by the sheep as the flock go farther and farther afield in search of fresher grass. More precisely, the sheep are led by a "head sheep", "someone among the flock whom the pastor also follows" (1986:130).

People often concentrate on the lesson of the parable at the expense of the imagery. To focus only on the message and sacrifice the image would be stripping it of its richness, the reality sought to be conveyed by the parable.

Another factor for the development of a sharp division between the clergy and the laity was the privileges extended to the clergy. Since the conversion of Constantine, the church enjoyed many favours. Among them, the bishops, priests and monks obtained important immunities and a whole series of enactments resulted in distinguishing the priests from the laity. His granting of enormous privileges to the clergy marked a turning point in the concept of power and authority in Christian ministry. We see a remarkable exaltation of the clergy, with royal patronage, in theory and practice far beyond anything known in New Testament times (Edwards 1987:56). The Eucharist in a fixed form, presided over by the bishop or his delegate in richly decorated attire became customary.

Ecclesiastical authority assumed power over life and death. In 384 a Spanish bishop, Priscillan was denounced as a heretic.

143

Together with him, four priests, a poet and a widow were put to death by the Emperor on the recommendation of the ecclesiastical authority. Only seventy years after the church gained freedom from persecution, state power was used by the clergy to deny life to the heretics. Ecclesiastical power was used to enforce the acceptance of Greek philosophical solutions to mysteries which the New Testament had left as mystery. Diverse theological movements which might have developed healthily were quickly branded as heretical, which if they did not disappear became more obstinate in isolation. It may be asked whether "the complete separation from heretics" was the necessary price of the defence of the true faith.

X. Clerical Intolerance Paves the Way for Secularisation

The intolerant attitude of the ecclesiastical authority coupled with the clerical interference in all aspects of life created great discontent among the people of Europe. This came to a head in the sixteenth century when Christianity was torn asunder by the Protestant Reformation, which was partly a religious movement and partly a political protest. During this period the churches had organised a piety which, while financially advantageous to the clergy had left many of the laity feeling remote and even alienated from the Church. There was a vacuum which the Reformation tried to fill religiously. But the reformation was also a political protest in the sense that Luther's religious revolt was sponsored by some of the German Princes because they resented the wealth of the clergy and in particular the constant financial demands of the papacy.

Luther tried to raise the status and role of the laity. In his work *To the Christian Nobility*, Luther rejected the hierarchical structure of the church and the distinction between clergy and laity. The principle of the universal priesthood of all believers, viewed as an essential teaching of the Word of God, provided a basis for insistence on the prominence of the laity in Protestant churches.

While the theological principle of the universal priesthood of all believers has been central to Protestantism, in practice, the ordained ministry is accorded a priority in keeping with the importance of its teaching, preaching and liturgical responsibilities for which special training and education are needed (Lusby 1989:264).

XI. Alienation of the Best Intellects Among the Laity

In the nineteenth century, the intolerant interference of the clergy in the affairs of the laity brought about a bitter conflict between European Christianity and modern science. There is no doubt that any new science could be in tension with an old religion. But the bitter opposition between Christianity and science does not seem to have been necessary. In the nineteenth century many of the great scientists were Christians and hence this might have been a time when religion and science could together inspire a spiritually and materially rich stable civilisation. Instead it witnessed a backlash of organised religion against the advance of science.

The Inquisition in Rome burned the pioneer scientist Giordano Bruno in 1600, and in 1633 Galileo was forced under the threat of torture never to teach again that "the earth moves and is not the centre of the universe".

The folly and arrogance of ecclesiastical power during the Renaissance had made religion appear as the enemy of realism, rationality and truth. The unfortunate confrontation of ecclesiastical and secular powers has resulted in the rupture of a unified vision, in which the spiritual and the temporal in human affairs seem to go their own way because the thinking laity could find no place in the church. They seem to be closer today, but not quite comfortable with each other yet. Stephen Hawking in his popular work, A Brief History of Time writes:

Throughout the 1970s I had been mainly studying black holes, but in 1981 my interest in questions about the origin and fate of the universe was reawakened when I attended a confer-

145

ence on cosmology organised by the Jesuits in the Vatican. The Catholic Church had made a bad mistake with Galileo when it tried to lay down the law on a question of science, declaring that the sun went round the earth. Now centuries later, it had decided to invite a number of experts, to advise it on cosmology. At the end of the conference the participants were granted an audience with the Pope. He told us that it was alright to study the evolution of the universe after the big bang, but we should not inquire into the big bang itself because that was the moment of Creation and therefore the work of God. I was glad then that he did not know the subject of the talk I had just given at the conference... I had no desire to share the fate of Galileo, with whom I feel a strong sense of identity, partly because of the coincidence of having been born exactly 300 years after his death (1995:122).

It shows that the tensions between the hierarchy and the scientists are not yet resolved. The paradox is that of all the civilisations in history, the Christian civilisation of Europe was the one that gave birth to modern science and democracy. Yet it turned its own children into secularists rather than religious people. According to Edwards, the most important explanation for the secularisation of Europe seems to be that "the clergy had a uniquely and excessively strong position — and abused it with arrogant folly" (1987:295).

XII. Rediscovery of the Rightful Place of the Laity in the Church

Duquesne argues that the existence of a clergy with a special style of life is harmful to the missionary activity of the church. This, according to him, follows logically from the Council of Trent which conceived the church as a fortress, with an organised clergy whose purpose was conservation of faith, not the conversion of souls (1969:156).

What is required may not be the dissolution of the clergy but the empowering of the laity to find their rightful place in the life and mission of the church. This requires a restructuring of posi-

146

tions. In the beginning the Christian priesthood followed the example of Christ who had opposed the Levitical society, the priestly caste. But gradually, as we have seen, the priest assumed the role of mediator between God and the world, a kind of 'heavenly sorcerer' (Duquesne 1969:71). Consequently, the church developed as a clerical society rather than as a people of God.

We are today rediscovering the New Testament concept of the church as the people of God wherein there is a basic equality of calling among all God's people. All God's people are called to be 'saints', to be priests, prophets and washers of one another's feet. There is no fundamental difference between Christian clergy and Christian laity, even though there is a difference in the function.

In the New Testament, as Congar points out, the word *hiereus* (priest, sacrificer) appears 30 times and the word *archiereus* more than one hundred and thirty times. They are used to denote either the priests of the Levitical order or the pagan priests. "Applied to Christian religion, the word *hiereus* is used only in speaking of Christ or the faithful. It is never applied to the ministers of the church's hierarchy" (1967:75). Our Lord had made it clear that in the Messianic community there would be no degree of power other than positions of service.

In the New Testament times there was no professional theological training nor specialist study for the training of the professional servants of the church. Theological study and discussion were there in plenty, but done by all the members of the church; merchants, slaves and women — in the home of one of the believers, and all made their contribution. Paul's letters were written not for the study of theological students, but for the members of his church. It was after Constantine, as we saw, that the church developed as a clerical institution rather than as the people of God.

Vatican II has rightly redefined the church as the 'people of God' and recognised that every lay person is a "witness and a living instrument of the mission of the Church" (*Lumen Gentium* 33). Though two decades have passed after the Council, the condition of the laity in the Catholic Church has undergone very little

147

change. Bishop Bosco Penha, chairman of the CBCI commission for laity, writing lately in the Examiner lamented: "The laity are a great treasure in the Church, but it is my impression that a very small percentage of them are involved in a regular basis in some service to the community, perhaps 2% to 5% . Is this a desirable state of affairs?" (1996:7).

One often gets the impression that the laity are now expected to do a little more for the church because there is such a shortage of clergy. But keen lay persons often keep away from the church and from regular worship. In worship the laity want to feel that they are doing something positive with their experience, while all that is asked of them is to be attentive. To worship fruitfully one must participate and contribute. The minister who is responsible for the conduct of worship must find the means for greater and more effective lay participation. In the same issue of the Examiner cited above, there is a cartoon of a priest in the vestry with four altar boys and a caption which reads: His idea of lay participation is having four altar boys at every mass. Though it is a caricature, the fact need not be far removed.

XIII. Lay Apostolate

The lay apostolate is not a substitute for clerical action: it is a specific evangelizing activity working through the environments and problems of life. Joseph Cardijn, the founder of the Young Christian Worker Movement was convinced of the decisive role of the lay apostolate in the future of the world and mission of the church. He remarks:

> And the more I have travelled through town and countries, the more clearly have I seen that the lay apostolate is the vital factor in the permanent confrontation of the Church with the needs of the present world. It is through laymen that the Church is in the world, and the more technical and unified our universe becomes, the more pressing will be the need for lay apostles (1964:17).

The task here is: how to make all men and women aware that they have a mission on earth which God himself has entrusted to them, a mission that is rooted in the realities of everyday life.

148

The mission of the laity consists in discovering the secular and divine dimension of humanity and linking it with the mystery of creation and redemption. He/she is called upon to give the temporal world its divine, religious and redemptive meaning in the whole of life and all the problems it sets — whether of science, technology, or social and human progress.

XIV. Giving Women Their Place in the Church

As we have seen in the earlier Christian communities women like Priscilla, Lydia, Tabita, Phoebe and others were prominent in their respective Christian communities. But with the rise of clericalism women were given the lowest place in the hierarchy of the church and today the fiercest discontent in the church is among women. It is not merely a fact of men oppressing women. We notice a pattern of structural violence which is given legitimisation by theology. According to the old Roman Hellenistic house code, women and slaves were possessions of men and so they were subject to them in all things. "Against the basic tendency of the earliest Christian inspiration, Christianity took over this pagan house code, brought it within the church and, moreover, gave it theological legitimisation" (Schillebeeckx 1985:236). Hence without much effort we can discover that the churches still carry with them a great deal of the baggage of the patriarchal understanding of authority rather than the partnership paradigm exhibited in Jesus' own critique of hierarchy and solidarity with the outcasts of society (Russell 1987:89).

XV. Theological Education

In the last hundred or so years, the theological education of the clergy has acquired a dominant and determining place in the life of the church. A tremendous deal of time and money is spent on the development of a huge apparatus, employing a large and carefully chosen staff, mainly to train men for the ministry of the church.

The service of these institutions can hardly be exaggerated. But the losses have been heavy. Gibbs and Morton point out three main drawbacks. First, they, more than any other single factor,

149

accentuate the denominational differences. Second, they detach the clergy from the ordinary life of the people. Taking the intending ministers away from a life shared with their contemporaries and shutting them up in special seminaries, often far removed geographically and always far removed psychologically from the life of the population, is not the best way to make them fit for the ministry in the fast changing world. It is directed toward sustaining a kind of life in the church that is already out of touch with the concrete life of the people. Third, they inflict damage on the image of the laity by the new professionalism of the clergy (1964:167ff).

In the theological colleges, the identification of ordination and professional service became complete and accepted. Their foundation left no place for the training of the laity in the service of the church. As the church felt the need for developing new forms of service, the curriculum of the theological colleges was enlarged to include subjects like pastoral psychology, pastoral counselling and so on. The danger is in its implication that such works can be done only by the clergy. The church has not begun to ask if such works are already being done by professionally trained lay persons. It prefers to train the clergy to do something amateurishly, rather than leave it to the professionally trained laity, giving the impression that the life and work of the church depends solely on the minister.

XVI. Conclusion

We, both clergy and laity, must remember that we have a common mission in the church. We are in the church not for our own sake but for the mission to which God has called us. Archbishop William Temple once said that "The church is the only great human society which exists for the sake of the people who are not its members" (Gibbs and Morton 1971:105).

The church exists for others. The church, the people of God, a called-out people, the *ekklesia* is a pilgrim people, whose duty is to call others to join in its march toward the kingdom of God. A minister must remember that his primary calling is in his baptism and not in his ordination. There is no hierarchy in the member-

150

ship of the church. This fundamental condition of common membership of the church, shared by the clergy and the laity alike, needs to find expression in the life, worship and mission of the church. Though society has changed radically in modern times, the structure and practice of the church by and large has remained in the pattern set in the Middle Ages, namely as a hierarchical, clerical society in which the laity have little responsibility. Thanks to the providential decline in the number of clergy and the better education of the laity, the church is now on the threshold of a new era of mutual understanding and co-operation among all its members as it was in the early stages of its existence.

References

Aguirre, Alphonso (1986) *Christ, Layman: Towards Renewal of Theology for the Laity in the Church*, Metro Manila: Asian Social Institute.

Branick, Vincent (1989) *The House Church in the Writings of Paul*, Delaware: Michael Glazier.

Cardijn, Joseph (1964) *Laymen into Action*, London: Geoffrey Chapman.

Congar, Yves (1967) *Priest and Layman*, London, Darton: Longman and Todd.

Deiss Lucien (comp.)(1967) *Early Sources of Liturgy*, London: Geoffrey Chapman.

Dunn, James D.G. (1988) *Romans: Word Biblical Commentary*, Dallas: Word Books.

Duquesne, Jaques (1969) *A Church Without Priests?*, (Trans. Bernard Mirchland), Toronto: The Macmillan Co.

Edwards, David L. (1987) *The Future of Christianity*, London: Hodder and Stoughton.

Gibbs, Mark and Morton, T. Ralph (1964) *God's Frozen People*, London: Fontana Books.

Gibbs, Mark and Morton, T. Ralph (1971) *God's Lively People: Christians in Tomorrow's World,* London: Fontana Books.

Hawking, Stephen (1995) *A Brief History of Time,* London: Bantam Books.

Lusby, Stanley F. (1989) *"Laity" in Eliade M. (ed.), Encyclopedia of Religion,* Vol.8, pp.425-429.

Oldham J.H. (1953) *Life is Commitment,* London: SCM Press.

Penha, Bosco Bishop (1996) *"Participation of Laity in the Life of the Church"* in *The Examiner,* 11: 7-9.

Russell, Letty M. (1987) *Household of Freedom: Authority in Feminist Theology,* Philadelphia: The Westminster Press.

Schillebeeckx, Edward (1982) *Ministry: A Case for Change,* London: SCM Press.

Schillebeeckx, Edward (1985) *The Church with a Human Face: A New and Expanded Theology of Ministry,* London: SCM Press.

Wagner, Walter H. (1994) *After the Apostles: Christianity in the Second Century,* Minneapolis: Fortress Press.

CHAPTER 8

Indian Missionary Spirituality

Mary Lobo*

I. Introduction

As interested as one is in exploring the spiritual dimension of life — and in this case of missionary life — writing about it is far from easy.

Some questions immediately come to mind. What do we mean by spirituality? How do we discover the stirring of the Spirit in the struggles and hopes of the people and in the processes of nature? In what way is the Spirit active in the various expressions of human cultures and in the creative theologies of the churches today? Is it feasible to talk of a specific missionary spirituality in the Christian churches and what is its thrust? What is the dialectic between missionary spirituality and the context?

In trying to answer these questions I would maintain that the Spirit is manifest in the way one responds to the situation: that is, in the quality of one's inner connectedness to the outer reality. In India this reality is characterised by massive poverty, ecological degradation and religious pluralism.Therefore the spirituality of those engaged in the church's mission — while being rooted in the gospel values — will have specific nuances marked by the Indian reality. This spirituality can open new pathways in the life and mission of the universal Church.

---

* *Mary Lobo, formerly Dean of Mater Dei, Goa, teaches missiology and is involved in Women Movements, especially among the marginalised in Bihar.*

II. Reflections on Spirituality

Spirituality refers to the life of the Spirit and spiritual life is human life open to the Transcendent. It is one's way of living, expressive of the inner integration between one's ultimate concerns, attitudes and the concrete existential responses to situations. Spirituality affects the quality of one's consciousness and this marks one's relationship to God, to one's self, to others and to nature.

Christian spirituality can be described as the daily life of the believing Christian. It is the way a person lives in a definite historical situation according to one's vision of faith and one's personal understanding of the Christian mystery. The first Christians were known as "people of the Way" (Acts 9:2; 22:4; 24:14) because of their way of life as disciples of Jesus (Reilly 1978:22-25).

Over the years there has been an incredibly vast output of writings on Christian spirituality. The five main trends in modern writings on spirituality have been precisely indicated by Joann Conn. These trends are: sustained attention to feminist issues; concern for the link between prayer and social justice; reliance on classical sources for answers to current questions; recognition of the value of developmental psychology and its understanding of "the self"; and agreement that experience is the most appropriate starting point (Conn 1990: 972-986).

1. Spirituality: A Cry for Life

In the mission context of India, lived experiences can be the bed-rock for deeper reflections on the subject. Relating to people and listening to their stories can draw one to a mine of spirituality. This is the place where we are taken by surprise and filled with a sense of wonder at the Spirit's action.

Recently Jamini Devi approached our Women's Organisation in Bodh Gaya, Bihar. She was deeply hurt, angry and physically ill. Her husband and in-laws had turned her out because she had given birth to two girls. We called for a meeting to negotiate between Jamini and her husband. Their parents too came along. In the presence of male relatives women in this culture remain silent. They are nothing. But to our amazement, Jamini spoke out, powerfully and in a spirited way! She exposed her grievances and demanded her rights. An agreement was finally reached. Her husband would immediately give her Rs. 3000/- for medical treatment while she stayed in her parent's home. She would later return to her husband's house, strongly determined to say "Yes" to life. The Spirit — women's spirit — cannot really be subdued.

Bodh Gaya is targeted to be a major centre for international tourism. Some months ago the road-side vendors and those running small shops were thrown out of the town in the drive for "beautification". Some of us NGOs and activists of people's movements were pained to see the plight of the people. They presented their demands at a *dharna* we organised at the Collectorate. There was a calm after that and soon our poor friends were out on the pavements again — selling their goods, first on the ground level on plastic sheets and a few days later on deal-wood boxes. Within a fortnight they had rebuilt their stalls, confident that they could earn a few Rupees each day. One could sense the surge of life, the daring spirit of the downtrodden when they were able to stand up and say "Yes" to life and "No" to oppression.

At Magadh Xerox, 22 year-old Shrikanth does a lot of my work. Last month he proudly told me that he was elected the local level BJP youth president. He asked me: "Were your ancestors Hindus?" I was uneasy and said: "Yes, maybe 400 years ago. But maybe 4,000 years ago my ancestors and yours were all tribals. And what if our present day tribals rose up and destroyed all our temples, churches and mosques?" The conversation led to a point where we both agreed that all Indians should be grateful and proud of their rich pluriform religious heritage; that all Indians should work for justice, truth and love as our religious teachers wanted us to do.

Such examples reveal that there is a spirituality implicit in all struggles for human dignity, freedom and harmony. The Spirit is manifest when people cry out against all that destroys or represses love and the fullness of life. Mission spirituality in India is a communion (community) with people, being together as we get in touch with the deep undercurrent of the Spirit's movements.

This implies an openness to the depth and mystery of events, things and people, going beyond surface realities, experiencing people's pain and hope. It means that we delve into realities — analytically and historically. Openness means we discern, evaluate and engage in critical activity — to open out new perspective on life, to unearth and contemplate new possibilities which bring hope and greater love into life (Rayan 1992:24).

Spirituality is also 'response-ability', a willingness to transform dehumanising reality. It is a call to conversion, a fundamental change of perspective — leading to action that can change structures both of the heart and of society. It implies taking a new road, living differently, because we are in solidarity with the poor of the earth. 'Response-ability' makes us vulnerable, questions our secure ideologies and leads us into the unknown in faith (Rayan 1992:25-26).

2. The Spirit-Mind-Body Continuum

At times there is uneasiness with the word 'spirituality' because the term is overlaid with other-worldly, dualistic connotations: matter versus spirit, body versus soul, earth versus heaven. Such disjointed understandings have resulted in alienation from our human roots, from the rest of nature and from the life-giving power of God. Today we use expressions like "spirituality of liberation", "spirituality of struggle", "earth-centred spirituality", "holistic spirituality" — implying that spirituality need not lead us away from life, but keeps us in touch with the life-energy that brings justice and compassion, harmony and hope here and now.

What is the experiential path to this harmony and wholeness, to a better life for humans and for the integrity of creation? Staying close to experience can simplify the search. Spirituality consists in awakening to the immediacy of the breath, knowing experientially that breath is life. In India, the practice of *pranayama* and similar techniques are the experiential method to energise one's being and to intensify and purify the consciousness (*citta*). *Prana* is the life principle, the breath of life which penetrates the whole universe.

All living things breathe. Oxygen or related elements are the stuff of life of birds and trees, of rocks and stars. Spirituality is the realisation that at this elemental level ALL IS ONE. All creation is permeated by the same life current and interdependence: relationship is the ground reality of life. Not just humans, but the forests, the rivers and the land, the myriad life forms are all to be held in reverence.

Spirituality includes the experience of feelings, the ebb and flow of life's energies in one's body — anger, joy — knowing that feelings are the dynamic life force that leads us into the vastness of LIFE itself, which is the ground of being.

3. The Spirit As the Feminine Ruah

To recapture the original power of the word 'spirit' in the Christian tradition we can examine the usage of the very important Hebrew term *ruah* in the Bible. *Ruah* refers to the breath of God, the wind, the air we breathe in our lungs, the energising presence of God, the seat of human experience. God is life-giver and breath comes from God (Gen 2:7) As a creative life-giving force, *ruah* originates in God (Gen 1:2; Is 42:1; Is 59:21; Ex 31:3; Ps 104:29-30). The Spirit impels humans to participate in God's power (Is 61:1; 32:15-19; Ez 3:26-27). *Ruah* is also vitally connected to human emotion (Ex 35:21; Is 19:3). Experientially we know how emotions affect the breath.

Ruah is a feminine concept while its Greek translation *pneuma* is neuter. Later the concept was transformed into the masculine with the Latin term *spiritus* and *spiritus sanctus* was personified as the third Person of the Trinity. In the process, the experiential base of the Hebrew *ruah* was robbed of its vitality.

This feminine nature of *ruah* is illustrated through images of birthing. Ezekiel 37 describes how Israel will be reborn after the darkness of the Exile. New life will emerge when the dry bones come to life again because of Yahweh's spirit — *ruah*. In the mighty wind of Pentecost (Acts 2:14) — it is the feminine *ruah* that is active when the young church is born. Though John writes in Greek and refers to the Spirit as *pneuma*, the maternal image of birthing is implied in John 3:5 — "Unless one is born of the water and the Spirit, one cannot enter the Kingdom of God" (Schungel-Straumann 1995:99-100).

Romans 8 is a foundation document for the spiritual life of those who believe in Christ. It explains how humans along with the whole of creation yearn for a fuller life, for a new earth: "The entire creation has been groaning in one great act of giving birth; and not only creation but all of us who possess the first fruits of the Spirit, we too groan inwardly as we wait for our bodies to be set free" (Rom 8:22-23). Here again the imagery of birth is revealing. The Spirit is the energy principle in this movement towards reconciliation, harmony and wholeness.

Experiencing the Spirit as feminine can be important in the emergence of a spiritual consciousness that is more holistic and unified. Such a consciousness "realises" the mutuality and interconnectedness of humans and all life forms present to each other in the same life stream. In this sense the non-male, earth-centred paradigms of feminist spirituality can be a valuable resource for the new earth community which is the only way to the future (Edwards 1989:19-20). Mission in depth needs to take these insights seriously.

III. Spirituality for Mission

· At this juncture we could raise a few issues concerning a specific spirituality for mission. As there is a plurality of spiritualities in the Christian tradition, we could affirm that those in the missionary outreach of the churches would need to develop a specific thrust in their spiritual vision. Basing his reflections on *Ad Gentes*, Yves Raguin explains how people called by vocation to carry out the church's mission are empowered with a specific charism different from other charisms in the Christian community. This impels the missionary to respond to challenges in "boundary situations" in a context (Raguin 1972:3).

Reilly, writing about mission on the six continents, refers to Rahner's concept of a diffused or diaspora character of Christianity. This has important implications for a spirituality of mission. Christian mission would need to highlight its sign role and enhance the quality of its witness to Kingdom values. Mission in the diaspora would essentially need to be prophetic. Boundary situations would no longer be geographic but would exist wherever there is a need for reconciliation between humans and groups (Reilly 1978:178-179). Mission spirituality would therefore unfold in the light of these Post-Vatican II missiological considerations.

IV. Mission Priorities in the Indian Situation

What is the Spirit's call in the diaspora situation in which missionaries find themselves in present day India? What spirituality and lifestyle do we need to cultivate so that we become transparent witnesses and authentic signs of God's Realm?

For the vision of God's Realm has to take shape in the Indian situation that is some times referred to as "creative chaos". On the one hand we have a new resurgence of cultures and religions as sources of identity for people. Yet on the other, religious fundamentalism and communalism are a source of tension in Indian life. There are signs of a vibrant democracy being born, with increasing participation by marginalised groups and regions. Yet we are haunted by the spectre of political instability and disintegration of the nation. Corruption erodes moral values. Oppressed groups (women, dalits and tribals) mobilise for human rights, liberation and fullness of life. But powerful interests spurred on by patriarchal, caste and hierarchical ideologies and strategies break these movements. Millions of poor people in villages and slums struggle for basic needs while the country is caught by global market forces promoting a consumer culture. Chipko, Theri and Narmada evoke hopes of sustainable development. Yet depleted forests, poisoned air in cities and aqua farming stands for devastation of the environment. What direction should missionary spirituality take when the Spirit promotes this "creative chaos"?

Ad Gentes 2 offers a vision: mission flows from the "fountain of love" which is God's own life, drawing us into communion so that God may be "ALL in all" (1 Cor 15:28). The missionary steeped in this vision is called and "sent" to share the experience of God's love in present-day India. This usually means that one leaves behind the security and power and the comfort culture that our institutions offer. Visible identity and structured modalities of functioning may have to be sacrificed if one wants to be "salt"

159

and "leaven", which are present in a milieu to give it a different quality. This vision might mean adopting a lifestyle where one can say in the words of Gandhi: "My life is a message".

Such a lifestyle would spring from a deep God-experience like that of Jesus. It would be marked by evangelical simplicity and transparency to the values of God's Realm. It would be expressed in the freedom to be present in new non-institutional ways with our fellow Indians — as co-workers and co-pilgrims, as people concerned for a new earth. The urge would be to further the values of God's Reign rather than church-centred interests.

Concrete modalities of missionary responses have been categorised in India under the liberation-inculturation-dialogue paradigm. What is the cutting edge of missionary spirituality in these modalities? The answer seems to lie in re-emphasising the prophetic dimension in the way one engages in liberation-inculturation-dialogue.

To elaborate: The struggle for justice invites all to work for the change of unjust structures. But missionary spirituality would impel one to prophetically challenge those responsible for structures calling them to a true conversion and reconciliation. So too, inculturation is the task of every local church and each Christian community should express the gospel in its own cultural forms. But the missionary approach would mean that the gospel poses a counter-cultural challenge and raises a prophetic voice against the limitations and negativities of the culture. Similarly, all people are called to live in harmony and engage in dialogue in a multi-religious culture. But missionary spirituality would lead us to question each others' lack of openness to God and to affirm that there is a prophetic impact on society when we join people of different faith to promote common human and spiritual values (Amaladoss 1990:14,60).

V. An Indian Missionary Spirituality

1. In Line with the Prophets

We have described how missionary spirituality in the complex Indian situation is marked by the prophetic stance which is characterised by reconciliation and compassion. What does the Bible have to say about the religious experiences of the prophets sent by God to open new possibilities among the people?

In Isaiah 42:1-4, the servant of Yahweh is endowed with a prophetic charism: "He shall bring forth justice to the nations, he will establish justice on the earth". The prophet will bring justice — *mispat* — which means he will pass judgement on the nations, because he is specially imbued with God's Spirit. The fourth Ebed Yahweh song (Is 52:13 — 53:12) indicates how the prophetic mission necessarily involves conflict and struggle: "Through his suffering my Servant will justify many". Isaiah 42:6 states that the Servant's call is in view of Yahweh's saving plan for humankind.

Jeremiah's pain was acute as he struggles to respond to the call: "Cursed be the day on which I was born" (Jer 20:14). But he experiences God's Spirit like "fire burning in the heart and I cannot endure it" (Jer 20:9). This urges him to launch out on his prophetic mission. Experience of God's presence and power reassures him: "But the Lord is with me as a dread warrior; therefore my persecutors will stumble, they will not overcome me" (Jer 20:11).

Through Ezekiel God tells the unrighteous to repent and live (Ez 18:32). The kind of life indicated here is one of communion with Yahweh. It is a life in the Spirit. Reference has been made to Ezekiel's vision of the dry bones becoming a mighty army (Ez 37). The prophet at God's insistence says: "Come from the four winds, O Breath, and breathe upon these slain that they may live" (v. 9ff). The spirit, breath, is clearly the source of life, it recreates life. The prophet is reassured by God's promise: "I will put a new spirit within you to give you a heart of flesh" (Ez 36:26). The prophet is to be intimately present to the human situation with a "heart of flesh". In the New Testament Jesus is the prophet *par excellence*. In Luke 4:18-19, Jesus announces that his mission reflects the messianic vision of Isaiah 61:1-2. "The Spirit of the Lord is upon me. He has sent me to bring the good news to the poor, to proclaim liberty to captives, and to the blind new sight, to set downtrodden free, to proclaim the Lord's year of favour". Jesus

161

will communicate life, hope and freedom because the Spirit empowers him.

New Testament women like Mary are also steeped in a prophetic spirituality. The Magnificat (Lk 1:46-55) summarises the surprising agenda for the new era. Mary prophetically announces the subversion of the established order in view of God's Realm. She is able to do this in the strength of her spirit which "rejoices in God my Saviour".

The early Christian missionary movement was initiated by daring, spirit-filled women who were prophets and missionaries (Acts 12:12-17; 17:4; 18:19-21; 21:8-9; Rom 16). These women were the first to announce and keep alive the good news that God's life-giving power was manifest in the resurrection of Jesus.

Acts 2:17ff reflect the words of the prophet Joel and tell us of a spirit-filled, egalitarian community of women and men committed to mission. "I will pour out my spirit on everyone. Your sons and daughters shall prophesy... both men and women... on them I will pour out my spirit on those days".

2. Discipleship: The Indian Way

At the heart of a missionary spirituality is the realisation that we are disciples of Jesus. But the thrust of discipleship is moulded by the Indian experience. How does the contemporary experience of living in India help us to understand Jesus, the giver of life?

The New Testament throws light on our situation. The christologies of the New Testament are clearly confessional, contextual and plural. At their heart lies an experience of Jesus, the impact he made on his first followers through his life and teaching, his death and resurrection. Each Christian community evolved its own understanding of Jesus from the experience of their own historical situation.

We could also gain insight from the way the churches have interpreted the Christ Event. The "Christ of faith" (in the dogmatic — liturgical formulae of the early churches) — originated in a climate of controversy. More recently we have the "Jesus of history" unearthed by historical criticism.

162

When all this ground is cleared, we are invited simply to rediscover the "Jesus of faith" as this is decisive for a vibrant Indian missionary spirituality. We can rediscover the "Jesus of faith" in the Gospels. These recount the way Jesus' first disciples experienced him.

Basically Jesus offered his disciples a new way to experience God. He himself communed with God in the silence of lonely places as well as in the midst of the crowd. The God-experience of Jesus sets him to change his pattern of life and launch out on his task as in Mark 1:14-15: "The time has come and God's Realm is at hand. Repent and believe the good news". Through miracles, teaching and companionship with the outcastes of society, Jesus announces the coming of God's Realm. His experience of God as "Abba", as unconditional love, (Lk 10:21; Mk 14:36; Jn 11:41) leads him to envisage a community of sisters and brothers brought together on the values of freedom, justice and companionship.

Jesus' experience of God's love frees him to reach out to those in need in solidarity and compassion. Liberated from fears, insecurities and compulsions, Jesus moves in the midst of people bringing healing and hope. He has an inner authority: charismatic and prophetic, not legal or institutional. He is able to question the oppressive role of the religious and political leaders of his time.

The experience of God's unconditional love leads him to different responses. In an unequal, unjust world love will take sides: "Blessed are you poor, woe to you rich". Solidarity with the powerless brings conflict with the rich. The disciple of Jesus today identifies and seeks solidarity with the outcaste and the poor. S/he knows the pain of dalit untouchability, the anger of women whose capabilities are blocked, the despair of tribals driven away from their homelands. As in the case of Jesus this solidarity invariably brings conflicts, oppression and death. But the resurrection of Jesus is God's final answer to our cry for life (Soares-Prabhu 1992:81).

But all this cannot be understood if there is no direct experience of involvement in the actual tasks of transformation of life. Our consciousness can open to the power of life and to the truth of the resurrection only when we struggle with others against the

163

forces that negate life (Soares-Prabhu 1992:83). When fragmented society is made whole, and when dalits, women or tribals organise to assert a new identity and claim their space in the vast expanse of reality, only then will we recognise the truth of the resurrection. These are foundational insights for an authentic Indian missionary spirituality.

The Indian way of following Jesus may not be the same as in countries of Africa or Latin America. The different nuances are rooted in the experience of relating to people from other great religious traditions of India. In this context, Jesus' experience of God as the absolute Mystery becomes especially significant. Indian religions teach us that this Mystery has a thousand names. This expresses the incredible richness of people's religious experience. God is beyond all these names and our limited perceptions and theologies. Therefore, in what way is Christianity unique? If there is something unique about Christianity, it is the way of Jesus: a way of solidarity and conflict as a path to fullness of life.

This uniqueness of Christianity must be lived and not talked about in abstract terms. Then our mission will be credible. At times we may be led to share this experience with our co-pilgrims as we yearn for a new earth and a new heaven or when we affirm as in the Isavasya Upanishad that "the whole world is pervaded by the glory of the Lord".

I have not chosen to explore the Indian, or rather, the sanskritised and elitist concepts in these reflections. One can write about *margas* and *darshanas*, *Atman* and *Brahman*, ashrams, *sadhana, moksha*, etc. In what way is this language meaningful for millions of our people at the periphery where the Spirit erupts very tangibly? Do we need to explain such terminology of the dominant stream when we realise that all Indians are called to move on to new human and spiritual realities; where Muslims, Christians, followers of primal religions, Hindus and Sikhs can find their true selves in a mutuality of relationships and service?

2. Indian Missionary Spirituality: An Alternative

Today India cannot afford to isolate itself in the emerging culture of global inter-dependence. Indian missionaries have an opportunity to make a specific contribution in this phenomenon. In the Christian churches cross-cultural mission is an established fact. In this communion between local churches, Indian missionaries have the privilege of offering unique gifts to enhance the life of the universal Church.

The reflections in these pages show how Indian missionary spirituality can contribute with two basic thrusts. Marked by a background of poverty, Indian missionary spirituality can radiate the power of the gospel, simplicity and radicalness. True inner freedom would be the outcome of voluntary poverty and detachment. The eagerness to collaborate with others for the sake of God's Realm and a non-violent approach in their involvements will be distinctive traits. As in the *anawim,* there will be a total reliance on God to fulfil God's promises. With this life style rooted in the Spirit, the consumer mono-culture growing in all parts of the world can be prophetically denounced.

Secondly, the experience of having been co-pilgrims with people of other faiths will be evident in greater interiority. An experimental approach to Christian living will be valued rather than dogmatic sureness. Indian missionary spirituality will be refined and deepened by the experience of religious reality in common with others. The only stance will be one of humble openness to the fullness of God beyond Christianity. This relentless quest for the ultimate Truth could lead to more creative theologies rather than christologies. As Reilly remarks, this might well be the hallmark of mission theology and spirituality for the future (Reilly 1978:205).

VI. Conclusion

This paper has outlined how the missionary call assumes a specific significance in the emerging contexts of India and the world. Mission is communion with the Spirit present and active, struggling for expression in the cry of people, in the groaning of creation for wholeness and in the human quest for the Transcendent.

As disciples of Jesus in India, missionaries have to discover the Jesus of faith and the vision of God's Realm that moved him.

165

This will give Indian missionary spirituality the real edge and the prophetic dynamism called for. Indian missionaries who live the Gospel from an experience of their context have important spiritual values to offer to the universal Church. Indian missionaries in pilgrimage with all people can affirm that ultimately God as Spirit is "Fullness from Fullness".

References

Amaladoss, Michael (1990) "Mission from Vatican II into the Coming Decade" in *Voices From the Third World*, December, pp.1-16.

Conn, Joann Wolski (1990) "Spirituality" in A. Komonchak, Collins & Lane (eds.), *New Dictionary of Theology*, pp. 972-986. Dublin: Gill & Macmillan.

Edwards, Felicity (1987) "Neo-Feminist Spirituality: An Evolutionary Perspective" in Virginia Fabella, *The Journal of Theology for Southern Africa*, March.

Rayan, Samuel (1992) "The Search for an Asian Spirituality of Liberation" in Virginia Fabella, Peter K.H. Lee & David Kwang-Sun Suh (eds.), *Asian Christian Spirituality*, New York: Orbis, pp. 11-30.

Raguin, Yves (1972) "Missionary Spirituality" in *EAPI*, Manila.

Reilly, Michael Collins (1978) *Spirituality for Mission*, New York: Orbis.

Schungel-Straumann, Helen (1995) "The Feminine Face of God" in *Concilium: The Many Faces of Divine*, London.

Soares-Prabhu, George (1992) "The Jesus of Faith" in *Voices from the Third World*, June, pp.46-9, Bangalore.

CHAPTER 9

Worship as Mission: Mission Within and Outside the Church

P. Surya Prakash*

I. Introduction

Both worship and mission are well known words in the Christian vocabulary. The two are among the most important concepts of Christian faith and practice. Traditionally the former refers to the function within the church; and the latter the function of the church to the outside. However, it has now been widely accepted that this division is artificial. Worship and mission belongs to the very nature and function of the church. Worship has been one of the foremost expressions of religious communities. Christianity is no exception to it. In fact one of the strong points of Christian faith and its practice has been its corporate worship. Worship has been described as service to God through the acts of praise and adoration of God. It also consists of confession of sin as well as confession of faith in God; praying for the needs of the world and reading and preaching of the Word of God as it is testified to in the Bible. Mission has been defined in many and varied ways in the course of the history of the church. It has been often identified with the Western Missions that came to India and other parts of the world preaching the gospel of Christ and doing many good works of healing and education etc. It has been associated with conversion from one of the religions into Christianity. But over

* P. Surya Prakash is Associate Professor of Preaching at the United Theological College, Bangalore.

the years this narrow understanding of mission has been changed into a much broader definition. Mission today is seen as a process of restoring wholeness and furthering fuller life to every creature. Establishment of a just society based on lasting peace and caring for the integrity of the whole creation is considered to be the true mission of the church. It is in this context that the relationship of worship and mission is discussed in this paper.

II. Relationship between Mission and Worship

What is the relationship between mission and worship so as to look at worship as mission? This is not the first time this question is being raised. J.G. Davis raised it in his book: *Worship and Mission* in 1966. This book was not about how to devise liturgical services for missionary gatherings, nor was it concerned with forms of worship in the mission fields. It was primarily a doctrinal study of the meaning of worship in terms of mission. J.G. Davis makes a critique of the traditional theological understanding of worship in one direction namely *inwardly*. It has been interpreted as that which builds up the church. He proposed another approach without denying the traditional one. It was suggested not as an alternative but as a compliment. He proposed to approach worship outwardly in terms of mission. Its contribution was to see worship in terms of the outward-looking dimension of the church.

III. The Old and New Testament Traditions of Worship

When we look at the vocation of Israel in the Old Testament accounts and the role of worship in relation to that vocation, we see that Israel's calling was to be a holy people (Lev 19:2). They were people whose life was fulfilled, then Israel becomes a light to the Gentiles (other nations). Israel becomes "a witness before the nations to Jaweh in order that the nations themselves may come to acknowledge his universal Lordship" (Davis 1973:319-320). The function of worship was to enable Israel to be a holy nation. Worship was a means of sanctification for the chosen people (Ex 19:6; Isa 2:2f). These passages make it clear

168

that Israel's calling is interpreted centripetally. Israel is not sent to the nations; instead they are to come to it, attracted by its life of worship and *bhakti* (devotion). Israel's worship was to be in a single place, namely Jerusalem, and all were expected to come there, including other nations. In contrast to this understanding, the New Testament understanding of the role of worship in the life of the church is the centrifugal one. The vocation of the church is to go out. It is to participate in the divine mission: "Go therefore and make disciples of all nations" (Mt 28:19). "As the Father has sent me, even so I send you" (Jn 20:21). "You shall be my witnesses to the ends of the earth" (Acts 1:8) in order that the nations may acknowledge the universal lordship of Christ. The function of worship in relation to this vocation is to celebrate God's action in the world and so to proclaim the Lord's death until he comes as it is reflected in the eating of the bread and the drinking the cup at the Eucharist in worship (1 Cor 11:26) (Davis 1973:320). The Church does not have a centre in a single place. God's encounter can take place anywhere in the everyday life. And the temple continues to exist not in a building but in a community living in the world (2 Cor 6:16). The church in its long history has tried to combine both the Old and New Testaments understanding of worship and defined worship in terms of gathering and sending. Worship has become an occasion for the coming together of the Christian community in order that its members may be strengthened to engage in mission in their life and work. Through the sharing in the life giving body and blood of Christ in the Eucharist, Christians are enabled to go out into the world for active missionary participation by their living. This understanding gives the impression that worship is a preparatory experience for mission. J.G. Davis argues that if mission and worship are to be truly united, the worshipping community must be understood within the context of mission. This has been amply proved in the former Soviet Union and in other East European countries, where gathering together for worship itself was seen as an expression of the mission of the church. The church existed basically on the liturgy and worship practices. Thus mission within and mission outside belong to the church as a whole.

169

IV. Mission and the Church

Mission is essentially an act of God, in which the church is called upon to participate. Worship is one of the means of participating in the mission of God. It is God centred in so far as we respond to God in it. In as much as it is directed to God, worship is also an act of reconciliation between God and people and people themselves. As J.G. Davis points out: "So worship and mission are not to be conceived as two distinct activities, the one theocentric and the other anthropocentric, both are aspects of a single divine activity in which, through Christ we are included. Personal commitment, worship, daily life, proclamation or witness are all parts of our response to Christ" (Davis 1966:71). The church is the church when it is participating in the mission of God. As J.G. Davis says, worship then is not a means to mission; nor is it a preparation for mission, since we worship in mission (Davis 1966:322). In Christ true mission and worship of God are revealed. Thus the church's mission and worship involve participation in Christ.

V. Mission as Response in Worship

Worship is the joyful celebration of life in the world. It is human response to what God has done and is doing in history. Luke 17 contains a narrative of Jesus' encounter with the ten lepers who plead for mercy and healing. Jesus accedes to their request and they are healed. One of them who is a Samaritan, recognises here the act of God and he worships — praising God with a loud voice, he falls on his face at Jesus' feet, giving him thanks (v.17). The act of worship takes place instantly in response to God's action of restoration to wholeness in the world in the form of expressing thanks and giving praise. Acts 4 records the incident how Peter and John are arrested; and after the trial before the Sanhedrin, they are eventually released. They then go to their friends and report what the chief priests and elders have said to them (Acts 4:23). The response of the group was to join in prayer. They worshipped together on the basis of the incident which has taken place in the world. Here we have worship interpreted from a centrifugal perspective. "Just as the world is understood to be the sphere of mission, so it is also the sphere of worship which is to be offered in terms of the Christian total existence (Davis 1966:323). The church never ceases to be in mission in the world whether it is preaching, serving or worshipping. The reality of the congregation materialises in the coming together of two or three (Mt 18:20). The early Christian communities gathered for worship celebrating the resurrection of Christ. The life of the faith communities was centred around worship (Acts 2:40-42).

VI. Mission as Celebration in Worship

Mission is not something that the church does. But it is the divine movement in which the church participates by virtue of its calling to be the Body of Christ. Thus the church's role is "to facilitate, to identify, and to participate in this movement, and the function of worship as response is to be understood within this totality" (Davis 1966:323). Worship is not merely a historical commemoration of what God has done in the past, but it is also a celebration of what God is doing in contemporary history through secular activities in the world. A more positive understanding has emerged now in our theological discussions that we recognise the signs of the divine activity in society at large for restoration to wholeness. Christian worship has been a celebration of the redemption of humanity in Christ. But now we have moved a step further and conceive worship as celebration of the divine redeeming act in the world at large, reaffirming the fact that God in Christ is reconciling the world to himself. In this sense worship can also be defined as "a social acknowledgement of the primacy of God's action" (Davis 1966:324). Unless worship and mission are united in this way, church services cannot but remain unreal and irrelevant to the present context. Our churches and chapels are to be part of the struggles in which people are involved. Worship and mission are to be understood primarily as being concerned with life in the world.

Our worship services as well as our service in different forms are directed toward our fellow human beings and in this way can be directed toward God. Jesus says: If I have washed your feet, you also ought to wash (not mine but) one another's feet (Jn 13:14).

Christ's action is aimed at us, while our action is to be aimed at our neighbour. Thus our mission of sharing in the divine activity cannot be divorced from worship. As J.G. Davis says "Worship is the celebration of a relationship which is always two-way; it is a relationship with the holy and man (and woman)" (Davis 1966:326). Our ritual action needs to be related to social change. The traditional forms need to be redefined and reinterpreted with the new ones which are meaningful within the present day secular and pluralist context. This would involve bringing in new perspectives such as, directing attention from the congregation itself to the wider society in which it lives; pointing to and manifesting unity within multiplicity; promoting empathy with strangers and encouraging new relationships; being critical of the social and political situation; and assisting the participants to accommodate to and cope with change (Davis 1966:332). The church needs to understand its worship theologically in the context of its total life in the world.

VII. Relationship of Liturgy of Baptism with Mission

In our Christian understanding baptism is a participation in Christ's death and resurrection (Rom 6:3); a rite in which the gift of the Holy Spirit is received (Acts 19); and a process of incorporation into the Body of Christ. Baptism makes us part of the community of believers. It identifies us as new creatures in Christ and heirs to the kingdom of God. Baptism enables conversion, pardoning and cleansing. It marks the beginning of a lifestyle of faith that witnesses to the reign of God. By the rite of baptism the people of God are sent into the world in mission, witness and service (cf. Henderson and others 1989:81).

Jesus' baptism marks an essential stage in his mission. Luke brings this out when he records how Jesus goes to the synagogue at Nazareth and declares: "Today this scripture has been fulfilled in your hearing" (Lk 4:18, 21). Christian baptism, through which we become partakers of the Spirit (Acts 2:38), is an anointing with the Spirit to equip the Christians for mission, thus bringing the baptized by the Spirit into the mission of God. Jesus' baptism was the occasion when he identified himself with those whom he had to serve; the same can be said of the Christians in their baptism (cf. Davis 1966:74). Jesus' baptism also points to the cross: "I have a baptism to be baptized with" (Lk 12:50). Paul connects Christian baptism closely with the death of Christ. This is interpreted mainly in terms of death to sin and rising to newness of life. Christ's death and resurrection mark the culmination of Jesus' mission and to interpret baptism in terms of participating in the death and resurrection of Jesus means, to be drawn into the mission of Jesus (Davis 1966:76). Baptism embodies the *kerygma* like the Eucharist since it is a proclamation of the Lord's death until he comes (1 Cor 11:26). It is a sacrament of identification, of suffering, of dying and of life poured out for others. We recognise that God calls people to fulfil God's purpose. The Gospel is for all but God calls some for participation in the mission. Baptism enables the baptized not to be taken out of the world but to be in the world and transform it by the power of the Holy Spirit.

VIII. The Relationship of the Liturgy of the Eucharist with Mission

There are different understandings of the Eucharist commonly called the Lord's Supper in the churches. Some see it as a sacrificial meal in remembrance of Christ (Catholic); and others as a memorial of what Christ has done (Protestant); and some others as the actual presence of Christ in the celebration of the Mass/Eucharist. The Eastern Orthodox tradition views the Eucharist as the context and the content of mission. The New Testament evidence shows that it is primarily a thanksgiving to God. It is the enactment of the whole drama of redemption. It is also an act of confession and penitence. Today it is seen as a meal for hungry people. It is a meal of liberation and it is a shared meal. The Eucharist leads to service of others and it is the meal of the kingdom (Henderson and others 1989:103). The Eucharist is the proclamation of the Lord's death until he comes (1 Cor 11:26) and it is related to showing forth the wonderful deeds of God (1 Pet 2:9). Both are at the heart of worship and mission. The concrete expression of the Eucharist in the life of the church is the communion in which the people of God share in the suffering of Christ through sharing in his ministry to the world. Unless the church embodies this self-giving in mission, through its eucharistic worship which celebrates the self-offering of Christ for the world, it ceases to follow its Master (cf. Davis 1966:103). That the Eucharist is to be understood in close relation to mission is shown in the New Testament by the accounts of the appearances of the risen Christ. These appearances are associated with meals on the one hand and commissioning for mission on the other. Oscar Cullmann has pointed out that these meals are links between the Lord's Last Supper and the Eucharist of the Church (cf. Cullmann 1958:5-23). Thus we can see that the Eucharist and mission are intimately bound together.

Worship strengthens the church for mission the two being related as cause and effect. Worship is also a means to the mission of the church both for itself and for the world in which the church is. When worship is mission, it is part of *missio Dei*. Then what does it mean to participate in God's mission is cultic acts? Worship needs to be seen as function of mission and mission as function of worship. This is an interdependent relationship.

IX. Baptism, Eucharist and Mission

Baptism enables participation in the covenant community and the Eucharist renews the covenant. Baptism initiates us into mission. The Eucharist reinforces the same. Baptism brings us into obedience of Christ and to his mission. The Eucharist renews our commitment to God and so to God's mission. Baptism is an initiation into the eschatological community and so is the Eucharist. Both are intimately related in this sense of the mission.

Worship and mission are aspects of a single totality and are constantly to be held together. What can be done about it? For many people worship and mission are separate entities. They need to see it as one. The answer is to be found in the systematic teaching of the missionary meaning of baptism and the Eucharist.

X. Indigenisation of Worship and Mission

Much has already been written on this subject both by Catholics and Protestants in India.[1] Indigenisation or inculturation of worship is closely linked with the mission of the church in relation to its worship and liturgy. Worship thought forms and expression of symbols and use images, when related to the ground realities of the worshippers, make worship contextual and appropriate. This in turn adds to the mission of the church (cf. Bosch 1991:447-455). We are all familiar with the developments in this century regarding the question of indigenisation of worship in India and elsewhere. We are also aware of the limitations of inculturation or adaptation. The plurality of cultures presupposes the plurality as well as forms of worship which take the local situation seriously.

XI. Reflection of Mission in the Acts of Worship

Each of the elements in worship depicts mission concerns. And most of the traditional elements in Christian worship have something to do with the mission of the church.

1. Prayer

We find in the early churches' traditions the community of the faithful were always found to be praying communities. They were praying not only for their needs but also for the needs of others especially for the work of mission and evangelism. The disciples devoted themselves to prayer (Acts 1:14). They had regular hours of prayer (Acts 3:1). The disciples consciously decided to devote themselves to prayer and proclamation (Acts 6:4). Coming together for the purpose of praying not only enabled the experience of fellowship but also an expression of solidarity with those for whom they offered prayers. They had appointed places for prayer (Acts 16:13). Paul constantly asks the churches to pray for his mission and ministry (1 Thess 3:10; Rom 12:12; 1 Cor 7:5; 2 Cor 1:11; Col 4:2).

---

[1] See special issue of *Banglore Theological Forum*, on indigenisation of worship, 1973 — 1. E. J. Lott (ed.) *Worship in Indian Context*, contains eight intercultural worship orders. The National, Catechetical and Liturgical Centre Bangalore has been doing poineering work in this area.

Jesus is portrayed by the Gospel writers being in prayer everyday (Mt 14:23; Mk 1:35; 6:46; Lk 5:16; 6:12). Jesus prays before healing (Mt 19:13). He asks the disciples to pray for their mission (Mt 9:38; Lk 10:2). Jesus insists on the necessity of prayer (Mk 9:29). Thus we see prayer playing a very important role in the life and mission of the church. "Prayer is not something seperate from mission", says J.G. Davis (1966:114). When the church prays it is engaged in mission. The prayer which Jesus teaches to the disciples is essentially a prayer of mission. The first four petitions speak of the mission of the church. Hallowed be your name: God's name is to be hallowed through the proclamation of the church. How can people glorify God's name if they have not heard of God? Yahweh's name is expected to be made known (Is 52:5-10). Israel is called upon to glory in the name of God (Ps 105:1-3). The church is called upon to showforth the excellencies of God in its life and witness (1 Pet 2:9). *Your Kingdom come* — The church is called upon to pray for the establishment of God's kingdom besides its own engagement for its realisation. This petition holds in balance the tension between the already or realised aspect of God's rule through the coming of Christ and the not yet of its total fulfilment. When we say this prayer we are affirming also our participation in the mission of God. *Your will be done on earth as it is in heaven.* This is another aspect that is closely linked with the mission of God. The author of the letter to the Hebrews speaks of Christ coming into the world as the fulfilment of Psalm 40:6-8 wherein it was expected that someone will do God's will. Christ's ministry is seen as an act of obedience to the divine will. Jesus subjects himself to the will of God to undertake the path of suffering which culminates in the cross (Lk 22:42). The fourth petition also has the mission perspective. *Give us today our daily bread:* The request is not just for Christians but for the whole of humanity. The Lord's prayer is essentially a prayer of mission.

2. Praise

Praise is also an aspect of mission. The author of Ephesians says that it is God's will that we should cause his glory to be praised (Eph 1:12). The goal of the mission of Christ, and of those who participate in his mission is that humanity may adore God. To share in Christ's mission is to join the praises by God's people. The real praise of God is the declaration of God's wonderful works (Is 43:21). Praise acclaims the acts of God in his mission to the world through Christ and the Spirit and the church. The church is called upon to offer a sacrifice of praise to God continually (Heb 13:15). Christian praise is a confession and affirmation of its faith in God through Christ before the world.

3. Thanksgiving

Christian thanksgiving is in response to what God has done (Heb 12:28; 2 Cor 9:15). It is through Jesus Christ that the Christians express their thanks to God (Rom 1:18; Col 3:17). Hence to be in Christ and to partake of his mission is to be giving thanks always (Eph 5:20; 2 Cor 4:15). Thanksgiving is both a liturgical act and a direction of living (Davis 1966:121)

4. Intercession

The church is called upon to make intercession for the world following the great intercessor of all, Jesus Christ (see Heb 3:1; Ex 28:21; Is 53:12). Intercession is a necessary element in worship. The intercession is essentially a presentation of subjects, of persons, of events, of needs, to the light and blessing of God. The difficulties of the church and of the world are exposed before God in order that the warmth of God's love may banish them. The intercession is a sacrificial and priestly prayer in which the church presents to God both persons and things that God may bless, strengthen and heal them (cf. Thurian 1960:59). Intercession is at the very heart of the liturgical act. As J.G. Davis says "Intercession is an act of love on behalf of others and so it is concerned with the restoration of love as the very life of the world — this is mission" (1966:123). The congregation takes part in mission through the intercession. Paul asks the churches for the work of ministry (Col 4:3; 2 Thess 3:1; Eph 6:19; Rom 8:26). Intercession and mission are two aspects of the Spirit's work in the world.

177

5. Confession of Faith

Confession of faith has always been a part of the Christian community ever since people began to accept Jesus as Lord (Rom 10:9). In the early church most probably every baptismal act was followed by confession of faith as we do it today. The content of confession always varied under the influence of preaching and witness of the church. The creeds of the church namely, the Apostles Creed and the Nicene Creed and others began to be formally used for confession of faith from the fifth or sixth century. The essence of confessional creeds has been the summary of the apostolic *kerygma* which declares what God has done in Christ. And the church is called upon to reflect by confession of mouth and putting into practice its perception of what God wants it to do. The confession of faith is not simply a summary of religious ideas but a statement of what we believe and confess as the church in response to what God has done and continues to do in Christ and in the Spirit.

6. Confession of Sin, Absolution and Peace

The worshippers' sense of unworthiness in the presence of God and the need for God's grace for forgiveness is yet another essential element in worship. Confession of our failures also involves our failures to be worthy witnesses of the gospel. The gospel offers forgiveness through the cross but also demands that we need to forgive one another. Forgiveness is not something we can achieve but God's forgiveness compels us to forgive others. Therefore, "forgive our tresspasses as we forgive those that tresspass against us" (see also Mt 6:14f). The liturgical forgiveness in the form of absolution has no meaning apart from forgiveness actualized in everyday life. The ministry of reconciliation, very much part of the mission of the church, is integrally related to confession and forgiveness of our sins against God and against one another. Our openness to forgive and accept each other is also a part of our ministry and mission. The ministry of the church has been called the ministry of reconciliation for God was in Christ reconciling the world unto himself (2 Cor 5:19).

In the symbolic exchange of peace and in the pronouncement of benediction, the ministry of reconciliation is again reflected. The kiss of peace (Rom 16:16; 1 Pet 5:14) is meant to bring reconciliation and peaceful relationships between one another. The exchange of peace goes back to the Hebrew greeting *shalom* on the one hand and the greeting of the risen Lord Jesus on the other. The word indicates righteousness, trust, fellowship and peaceful relationships. Shalom is not something that can be objectified nor is it something that can be internalised (peace of mind). It is a social happening, an event in inter-personal relationships. It cannot be reduced to a simple formula but has to be worked out in actual situations. The ultimate aim of mission is the establishment of shalom. Thus the element of the expression of peace or kiss of peace in worship is also very much related to the mission of the church.

7. The Readings and the Sermon

The Bible being the testimony of God's involvement with people in God's creation is itself a mission document in the sense that it bears witness to *missio Dei* in the past. When by faith it is accepted as the Scriptures it becomes a summons to participate in God's mission in the present. The historical facts become contemporary reality. To know what God has done in the past is to reflect upon what God is doing in the present. The understanding of the word of God through the preaching of the church enables us to discern what God is telling us today. The preaching of the sermon is an exposition of the word of God that it may become the living word. Preaching set within worship incorporates the mission of God through the believing community being challenged and edified. Proclamation and mission always go together. As H.H. Farmer points out: "Even in instruction, edification and confirming of the saints the note of claim and summons (found in *kerygma*) should not be absent" (Farmer 1942:67). Thus every sermon is expected to have a note of *kerygma* with the missionary dimension. Sermon is also a call to mission and service. The congregation is encouraged to fulfil its missionary call.

8. The Offertory

The offertory is an essential element in Christian worship. It is meant not only for the self-support of the congregation but also its outreach programmes which fall under the category of mission. Paul was always concerned that churches help and support one another. He writes to the Corinthian Christians how the money is to be collected (1 Cor 16:1-4). He urges them to give liberally (2 Cor 8-9). He compliments the Philippian Christians on their financial help (Phil 4:15f). He describes to the Roman Christians the efforts that are being made for helping the churches in need (Rom 15:26). He considers Christian giving an essential element in *koinonia* (2 Cor 9:13, Rom 15:26). Sharing is integral to a community of the faithful. The Church of South India has chosen for its *jubilee biennium* the theme: "Sharing and Growing Together in Unity". Paul not only calls this contribution *koinonia* but also grace (2 Cor 8-9). Giving money is an expression of self-giving. Christian giving is a response to what God has given to us. That is the service of *diakonia*. Mission involves not only the preaching of the word, but also the witness of the life of *koinonia* and *diakonia*. Both are intrinsically integral to mission and ministry.

9. The Announcements and the Benediction

Invariably church services contain notices or announcements in relation to its activities and needs. The members are called upon to actively participate in the ministry. Thus the notices also become a means to mission. At the end of the services the members are sent into the world with a blessing to be witnesses. Therefore benedictions become the channel whereby the congregations are encouraged to go out as faithful witnesses with God's blessings.

There are practical implementations for the life of the church. There is a great deal of talk about the renewal of the church for mission. We hear of liturgical renewal for reformation and transformation of the church. Both these are the two aspects of the church. They are not independent of each other, but interdependent. Renewal of the church and re-vitalisation of the liturgy are integrally related. The church exists in mission and it is only in mission that it can be renewed. Worship and mission are twin aspects of this reality. When the church prays it is engaged in mission.

XII. Conclusion:
Mission Within and Outside the Church

Jesus calls the disciples so that they might be with him and be sent out on a mission to preach, to heal the sick and to cast out the demons. Mission begins with us. In spite of tremendous advances in science and technology and enormous facilities to understand human nature and creation, people have not learnt to live together. Our situation calls for a new orientation to life based on certain values and not on things alone. An endurable value system can only be found in God based on the gospel. We need a mission within the church. In the context of growing individualism and selfishness, we need to think of communities turning from self-centredness to God and community-centredness. It is out of a life of sharing and caring and a sustaining community that a community of witnessing comes. We cannot carry on mission of the gospel unless we are possessed by the gospel. It is out of the experience of living in a community of caring, sharing and sustaining that a community of mission grows. Worship plays an important role providing the content and the context for the mission of the church in the world.

References

Davis, J.G. (1966) *Worship and Mission*, London: SCM Press.

Davis, J.G. (1973) *Everyday God*, London: S.C.M Press.

Henderson, J. Frank and Others (1989) *Liturgy, Justice and the Reign of God*, Paulist Press.

Cullmann, O. (1958) *Essays on the Lord's Supper*, Richmond: John Knox.

Bosch, David J. (1991) *Transforming Mission: Paradigm Shifts in Theology of Mission*, N.Y.: Orbis Books.

Farmer, H.H. (1942) *The Servant of the Word*.

Frank S. Cellier, Frank S. (ed.) (1964) *Liturgy is Mission*, New York: Seabury Press.

Lott, E.J. (ed.) (1973) *Worship in Indian Context*.

Samuel Amirtham "The Significance of Lay Participation in Christian Ministry" in S. Vasantha Kumar (ed.), *Call to Ministry and Mission: Essays in Honour of Bishop K.E. Gill*.

Girwin van Leeuwen (1991) "Liturgy, the Struggle for Relevance Continues", in Paul Puthanangady (ed.), *Church in India — Institution or Movement*, pp.25-35, Bangalore: NBCLC.

Paul Puthanangady (ed.) (1986) *Popular Devotions in India*, Bangalore: NBCLC.

Paul Puthanangady (ed.) (1989) *Sharing Worship*, Bangalore: NBCLC.

John Leach (1989) *Liturgy and Liberty: Combining the Best of the Old with the Best of the New in Worship*.

LWF Studies (1994) *Worship and Culture in Dialogue*.

Thurian, M. (1960) *The Eucharistic Memorial*, London.

CHAPTER 10

Dialogue as Evangelizing Mission

Joy Thomas*

I. Introduction

Thirty one years ago the Second Vatican Council closed calling the Catholic Church to consider dialogue as part of the Church's evangelizing mission in a multi-religious context. The theological foundation of the Church's action is the awareness that God is the source of humankind's common origin and all share God as their common destiny (NA 1). The declaration *Nostra Aetate* (NA) urges the missionaries not to discriminate or destroy the different religions (NA 5) as they contribute to peoples' search for meaning (NA 2,3). Vatican II placed before us the missionary challenge to preserve from destruction the good found sown in the minds and hearts of everyone or in the rites and customs of peoples (LG 17). It urges the missionaries to enter into discussion and collaboration with the members of other religions. The focus of this call was clarified twenty years later with the publication of *The Attitude of the Church Towards the Followers of Other Religions* as a voyage of mutual discovery or rather a common pilgrimage. All believers are invited "to walk together towards truth and to work together in projects of common concern" (DM 13).

Christianity and non-Christian religions from the thirties to the fifties, the Word of God and the living faiths from the

---

* *Joy Thomas holds a doctorate in missiology and is the Programme Director of Ishvani Kendra, the Institute of Missiology and Communications. He is the Central Mission Procurator of the Divine Word Missionaries in India.*

seventies onwards have been a concern in the ecumenical movement. The Assembly of the International Missionary Council at Madras, in 1938, was pre-occupied with the study of the Christian message in a non-Christian world. At its Assembly in Whitby, Ontario, in 1947, the IMC set itself to discover the relevance of the gospel to the world recovering from war. The IMC Assembly in Ghana, in 1958, which decided in favour of the integration of the IMC with the WCC, ratified the study of *The Word of God and the Living Faiths of Men* (J. Van der Bent 1986: 45).

Every one is called to contribute to the building up of the Kingdom of God, as no one has the monopoly of initiatives. Hence the focus in this paper is on dialogue of life and action leading all religious institutes and movements to meet and to enter into collaborative ministries which are referred to as "kingdom ministries" in order to promote various dimensions of the kingdom, namely, truth, life, holiness, justice, love and peace.

II. Forms of Dialogue

In the context of India, dialogue is part and parcel of every aspect of life. In the village where I grew up, Hindus, Christians and Muslims lived in harmony and peace. Caring and sharing were tangibly felt on feast days. The special festive eatables were exchanged among the three communities. In fact my close friends in school were Kumaran, a Hindu boy, and Konthalam, a Muslim boy. We went to school together and even attended one another's worship on important feast days. Solidarity and fellowship were at its best during major family events like birth, marriage and death.

For the sake of convenience, it is customary to identify different forms of inter-religious dialogue. In books and discussions we come across four types:

1. Dialogue of life,
2. Dialogue of action,
3. Dialogue of specialists,
4. Dialogue of religious experience.

184

All these forms can be brought under the single title "Dialogue of Life" in our context, as the Indian way of life is dialogical. Such sharp divisions into different forms only impoverish dialogue as the evangelizing mission of the Church in India today. As Cardinal Newman says, "our statements die the death of thousand distinctions". For the last thirty years the Church has experimented with all forms of dialogue, but these efforts have just remained as experiments. It has failed to create interest among Christians. And the majority of the people of other religions look upon such efforts suspiciously. The tangible results are structures at local, national and international levels. The CBCI has a Commission for Dialogue, which is linked with Diocesan Commissions. At the Asian level Bishops' Institute for Inter-religious Affairs (BIRA) was established in 1979. And in Rome there is a Pontifical Council for Inter-religious Dialogue (1988), which was established as the Secretariat for Non-Christians in 1964 by Paul VI. The World Council of Churches has its office on Dialogue with people of living Faiths.

The religious enquiry and the consequent elimination of prejudice, intolerance and misunderstandings Pope John Paul II is talking about in *Redemptoris Missio* is aimed at "spiritual fruits" (RM 56). Such statements are made in the context of Europe where other religions are concepts in books and not a living reality (at least in the past). In the multi-religious situation of Asia, no one has any choice but to enter into a process of dialogue all through life. The basis of dialogue is clarified in the Kandy Consultation on Christian dialogue with people of other faiths:

> As our dialogue with people of other faiths develops, we may gain light regarding the place held by other religious traditions in God's purposes for them and for us; this is a question which cannot be answered a priori or academically, but must continue to engage our earnest study and reflection (J. Van de Bent 1986:46).

No one needs to be taught the techniques of dialogue for everyone develops their own way of doing it as they are nurtured in their society. When love is the foundation of dialogue, it just

185

happens in society and, when love fails it results in riots and other bitter consequences. As action follows life, Dialogue of Action is the natural consequence of Dialogue of Life, in response to natural disasters like floods or famine and other situations of distress like communal disturbances in our country. Such operations can easily be coordinated by committed Christians to allow people of different religions to work together in a spirit of acceptance and respect. These involvements are the *Kingdom ministries* tangibly communicating the Good News: "God is with us and He loves us".

The "seeds of the Word" found sown in the religions allow dialogue to take place spontaneously. Hence, every dialogue is triangular. Besides the dialogue partners the Holy Spirit is at work not only among Christians but also beyond the visible boundaries of the Church.

III. Evangelizing or 'Ad Gentes' Mission

Pope Paul VI is known as the Pope of dialogue. In his encyclical *Ecclesiam Suam* (1964) he calls for a renewal in the Church and a movement toward communication in dialogue. Pope John Paul II in his missionary encyclical *Redemptoris Missio* states, "Inter-religious dialogue is part of the evangelizing mission of the Church" (RM 55). Both dialogue and proclamation belongs to the Church's evangelizing mission in the sense that inter-religious dialogue becomes just one of the integral elements of mission like inculturation and promotion of the human person (RM 44).

However, both Paul VI and John Paul II insist on the importance of proclamation. The former says, "Our dialogue must not weaken our attachment to our faith" (ES 5). The latter speaks of the urgency and permanent validity of 'mission ad gentes' because the mission of Jesus Christ is "still very far from completion" (RM 1) and not only that "the number of those who do not know Christ and who do not belong to the Church is constantly on the increase. Indeed, since the end of the Council it has almost doubled" (RM 3). The encyclical emphasizes that Jesus Christ is the one Saviour of all in whom God's revelation becomes definitive and complete (RM 5). Hence its main focus is the centrality of proclamation and the permanent priority of the evangelizing mission or 'ad gentes' mission (RM 44).

John Paul II reminds the church that dialogue "should be conducted and implemented with the conviction that the Church is the ordinary means of salvation and that *she alone* possesses the fullness of the means of salvation" (RM 55). Dialogue does not dispense with evangelization. "One cannot, in the name of these ways, slow down or abandon missionary activity" (John Paul II 1995: 11). Such statements betray the Church's fundamentalistic attitude and tend to downplay the attitude of respect and friendship which should permeate all those activities, including mission as dialogue, that constitute the evangelizing mission of the Church. Hence, justified is the suspicion of people of other Faiths that Christian dialogue is nothing but a subtle strategy of the Church's evangelizing mission leading to conversion.

IV. Dialogue and Proclamation

The immediate object of our dialogue, according to *Ecclesiam Suam* is "conversion to the true faith" (ES 79). Hence, dialogue remains "oriented towards proclamation" (DP 82). Paul VI says that "there is no true evangelization if the name, the teaching, the life, the promise, the Kingdom and the mystery of Jesus of Nazareth, the Son of God are not proclaimed" (EN 22). "Preaching, the verbal proclamation of a message, is always indispensable" (EN 42). In all Church documents and statements of the Popes, explicit proclamation of the gospel of Jesus Christ always has priority over dialogue and "true inter-religious dialogue on the part of the Christian supposes the desire to make Jesus Christ better known, recognized and loved" (DP 77). It is justified by proposing the basic principle that in dialogue neither party "lay aside their respective religious convictions" (DP 48).

Proclamation, in the Christian context is the sharing of the Good News that God loves us. It must always be made in the spirit of dialogue. What the Church does is to impress upon everyone that explicit proclamation is not to be considered opposed to inter-religious dialogue. At the same time this dialogue cannot be understood as an alternative to proclamation. The Asian theological insight, that mission amongst the great religious traditions is dialogue, is seen by the Church as belittling the importance of explicit proclamation. The Catholic Church insists that under no circumstances could or should direct and explicit proclamation of the mystery of Christ be replaced. Dialogue can include proclamation in the sense that it must be undertaken by those who have good news to share. As genuine love is mutually transformative, dialogue as an expression of love involves the risk of one partner being changed by the other.

Dialogue with people of other faiths is seen in traditional Church circles as a betrayal of mission. Such concerns are expressed several times in the documents of the Catholic Church's Magisterium. "There are those who would seem to think, erroneously, that in the Church's mission today dialogue should simply replace proclamation" (DP 4). The latest expression of such a concern is seen in *Redemptoris Missio* where the Pope says that "some people wonder: Is the missionary work among non-Christians still relevant? Has it not been replaced by inter-religious dialogue?... Is it not possible to attain salvation in any religion? Why then should there be missionary activity" (RM 4)? Even in difficult situations, in the midst of challenge and opposition from followers of other religions, John Paul calls for sincere witness to Christ and generous service because "dialogue is a path towards the Kingdom and will certainly bear fruit, even if the times and seasons are known only to the Father" (RM 57).

V. Dialogue and Conversion

The document of the Pontifical Council for Inter-Religious Dialogue and of the Congregation for the Evangelization of Peoples, *Dialogue and Proclamation*, states that the object of inter-religious dialogue is "a deeper conversion of all towards God" (DP 41). The bishops of Asia have come to the realization that "sincere and authentic dialogue does not have for its objective the conversion of the other" (BIRA III 1982:120 N.4). And Pope John

Paul II states that "those engaged in dialogue must be consistent with their own religious traditions and convictions, and be open to understanding those of the other party without pretense or close-mindedness, but with truth, humility and frankness, knowing that dialogue can enrich each side" (RM 56).

But we are reminded that dialogue "does not constitute the whole mission of the Church, that it cannot simply replace proclamation, but remains oriented towards proclamation" (DP 82). It is through proclamation that "the dynamic process of the Church's evangelizing mission reaches its climax and its fulness" (DP 82). So the Church holds on to the principle that proclamation "has Christian conversion as its aim: a complete and sincere adherence to Christ and his Gospel through faith" (RM 46).

VI. Dialogue and Inculturation

What comes through the statements of the Popes and Magisterium is that ours is the true faith. And this basic attitude of superiority is obvious in the documents of Vatican II and *Redemptoris Missio*. Dialogue is neither a technique nor a strategy as our RSS friends read into these Church statements, but rather is a real task of everyone, both believers and unbelievers. In our world today nobody can be isolated or separated. Even for understanding ourselves better as Christians, dialogue is indispensable. Comparison and contrast help us to have deeper insights into truth. When someone else does and thinks differently, we understand deeply what we do and think.

Dialogue deepens our understanding of God. As every religion has only a partial understanding, no religion can claim the monopoly of Truth. Panikkar and other Asian theologians are of the opinion that in a spirit of true dialogue we must recognize the relativity and interdependence of different religions. Faith is formed from religious experiences not adequately understood. Beliefs and consequently doctrines are expressions of faith in a particular cultural context. Beliefs are concrete expressions and, therefore, limited and have a limited value. Here the Buddha's story of the blind people and the elephant is very pertinent. The perception of each one has to be shared to come to the full un-

189

derstanding of an elephant. So too sharing of different religious experiences snowballs into greater insights about the Absolute and makes the Church more Catholic, enriching her with the values of other human and religious traditions.

Our people must be educated and encouraged for *communicatio in sacris*. Such participation in the sacred rites of the other like *puja, prasad*, etc. helps one to experience what people of other religious traditions experience. We have to go beyond mere presence to partaking in *prasad* and *puja* itself. Participation in a Hindu *puja* helps a Christian to experience what Hindus are experiencing.

Participating in the *Satyanarayan Puja*, for example, with the intention of worshipping the Supreme Being, helps one to understand the Supreme Reality as Vishnu. It is not mere study that transforms one rather the religious experience. Hence, inter-religious dialogue should include partaking in the religious experience of the other not mere study or discussions. There is some value in all religious traditions. They can touch and change me if they are assimilated. If properly understood, it can also be said that such experiences would make me "less of a Christian" and would help me to realize that my own beliefs and practices cannot be seen as absolute. Perhaps, Panikkar points to this experience when he writes, "I 'left' as a Christian, 'found' myself a Hindu and 'returned' a Buddhist without ever having ceased to be a Christian" (Panikkar 1973:42).

The so called good and faithful Christians consider *communicatio in sacris* as really sinful and wrong. Every time I participated in the religious functions of my childhood friends Kumaran and Konthalam, my grandparents forced me to confess those sins! Today this problem has moved from village homes to city offices. Can one accept *prasad* from devout Hindu colleagues in the office on their feast days? If one refuses to do so and to participate in the liturgy of the other, he or she is not sharing life with the colleagues at work!

VII. Conclusion

In the context of life, the threat of communalism shows how

religions in India are exploited by vested interests. People belonging to different religions can live together in one civic society pursuing common human values on which they agree. This has to be demonstrated through dialogue, which is essential to dispel negative attitudes to people of other faiths. Christianity today is called to play this prophetic role, challenging and inspiring everyone in the country through dialogue as its evangelizing mission to be effective and relevant. The very word 'evangelisation' means 'gospelisation', making gospel or Christian values known. Hence, this calls for both sharing through Evangelization and enrichment through dialogue. Such mutual enrichment in a sense of balance truly demonstrates the Gita ideal *lokasangraha* (working for the welfare of the world), which is the challenge of dialogue today.

A silver lining of hope is provided by the WCC Guidelines on Dialogue with People of Living Faiths and Ideologies:

> To enter into dialogue requires an opening of the mind and heart to others. It is an undertaking which requires risk as well as a deep sense of vocation. It is impossible without sensitivity to the richly varied life of humankind. This opening, this risk, this vocation, this sensitivity are at the heart of the ecumenical movement and in the deepest currents of the life of the churches. It is therefore with a commitment to the importance of dialogue for the member churches of the WCC that the Central Committee offers this Statement and these Guidelines to the churches (WCC:1979).

Pope John Paul himself suggests that "many missionaries and Christian communities find in the difficult and often misunderstood path of dialogue their only way of bearing sincere witness to Christ and offering generous service to others" (RM 570). But the traditional exclusivistic and fundamentalistic attitude has come to stay in the Church for every Christian is warned that "the Church is the ordinary means of salvation and that *she alone* possesses the fullness of the means of salvation" (RM 55). From such a position of superiority the practice of dialogue becomes "patronizing mission".

The evangelizing mission of the Church, if it is true to its founder, is a mission of service to humanity. The mission manifesto of Jesus is the mission of the Servant of Yahweh (Lk 4:18). The Gospels are a witness to the idea of universalism in the mission of Jesus (Mt 2:1ff; 4:15-17; 6:5-13; 22:1-10; 28:19; Lk 2:10, 14, 23; 3:1-6; 7:1-10; 13:28; 14:16-24; 24:46ff; Mk 5:1-20). The story of the Syro-Phoenician woman in Mark 7:24-31 is a good illustration, besides others, of his openness to a person of a different faith. In the gospel of Mark, Jesus is presented as opening his mission activity to a variety of people from Galilee, Idumea, Tyre, Sidon and beyond the Jordan. The basic concern of Jesus was service and Mark captures it in His words to the Syro-Phoenician woman, "you may go your way" (Mk 7:29).

The disciples of Jesus, therefore, should not be a party to religious distinctions. His disciples are invited to a religion of service, when he exhorts them, "if I, your Lord and Teacher, have washed your feet, you also ought to wash one another's feet" (Jn 13:14). John's consciousness, that "what God requires of all is love", is summarized in his letters. Christian dialogue as evangelizing mission can neither be exclusivistic nor inclusivistic but service-oriented. In other words, true Christian Mission today in the context of many religions is *kenotic* service. If all religions are engaged in the mission of service to humanity, the basis for dialogue will be real (Cf Wilfred 1991: 271).

References

LG: *Lumen Gentium*, Constitution of the Second Vatican Council on the Church, 1964.

ES: *Ecclesiam Suam*, Encyclical of Paul VI, 1964.

NA: *Nostra Aetate*, Declaration of the Second Vatican Council on Religions, 1965.

EN: *Evangelii Nuntiandi*, Apostolic Exhortation of Paul VI, 1975.

DM: *Dialogue and Mission*, Document of the Secretariat for Non-Christians, 1984.

RM: *Redemptoris Missio*, John Paul II's Missionary Encyclical, 1990.

DP: *Dialogue and Proclamation*, Document of the Pontifical Council for Dialogue, 1991.

WCC: *World Council of Churches*, Guidelines on Dialogue with People of Living Faiths and Ideologies, Geneva, WCC, 1979.

Study Encounter, Vol.III, No.2, 1967, pp. 53-55.

RAYMOND PANIKKAR, *The Trinity and the Religious Experience of Man,* Maryknoll, Orbis Books, 1973.

FELIX WILFRED, *Sunset in the East*, Chair of Christianity, Madras, 1991.

JOHN PAUL II, *The Goal of Missionary Activity,* L'Osservatore Romano, 10 May 1995.

J.VAN der BENT, *Vital Ecumenical Concerns: Sixteen Documentary Surveys*, World Council of Churches, Geneva, 1986.

CHAPTER 11

Mission as Church Growth

James Chacko*

I. Introduction

The first task of the Church is to call all humanity to reconciliation with God. The Church Growth Movement, therefore, was right in recalling the Church to awareness of this priority. As we consider the case of 'Mission as Church Growth', we do so through an assessment of the strength and weakness of Church Growth Theory for the mission of the Church.

It begins from an evangelical viewpoint with primary reference to biblical criteria. Although it is the theory as such which is under evaluation, this of necessity is read in terms of its meaning to proponents and practitioners. Various contributions of Church Growth Theory to the development of the science of missions are identified but numerous problems and inconsistencies are also raised.

"That the blood of the martyrs is the seed of the Church" (Tertulian, c.200 AD) is among the earliest of attempts to account for the growth of the church, each reflecting something of its era. An evaluation of Church Growth Theory will require some understanding of Church Growth Movement. Beginning with its own essential definition:

* James Chacko is a Lecturer in missiology and the Registrar at COTR Theological Seminary, Visakhapatnam. He is also the Executive Secretary of the Association International Mission Service (AIMS-India) and a member of the Fellowship of Indian Missiologists.

Church Growth is that science which... strives to combine the eternal theological principles of God's word concerning the expansion of the church with the best insights of contemporary social and behavioral sciences, employing as its initial frame of reference the foundational work done by Donald McGavran (Wagner 1980:14).

As the ideas of Church Growth have developed, so a very large number of so-called 'principles' has been recognized. Peter Wagner, one of the principal proponents of McGavran's ideas, makes reference to sixty-seven such principles ascribed to McGavran, fifty-one principles ascribed to himself, and a total of 146 principles so far proposed. However, Church Growth is not just concerned about developing principles but is a concern for the Kingdom growth.

II. The Development of Church Growth Theory

The Church Growth Movement finds its roots in India. In the 1930's the research was conducted under the auspices of International Missionary Council and the National Christian Council of India by a Methodist Bishop J. Waskam Picket. His findings were published in the book *Christian Mass Movement* (Pickett 1933). However, the foundations of Church Growth Theory were laid in the 1955 publication of McGavran's *The Bridges of God* (McGavran 1955) from which emerged the three pillars of Church Growth Theory.

McGavran's fundamental observation was that the church grows most effectively through people movements rather than individual accessions. Considering also that people prefer to become Christians without crossing cultural barriers, Church Growth Theory takes as its *first principle* the propagation of churches in "Homogeneous Units", a process in which the social sciences assist (McGavran 1955:122). A *second* priority outlined by McGavran is toward "discipling" rather than "perfecting" (McGavran 1955:13). Setting numerical growth of the church as the goal of mission a *third* principle is that "the church ought to concentrate its resources in those areas that show growing 'receptivity' to Christianity (McGavran 1955:119).

III. Criteria for Assessing Strengths and Weaknesses

1. Absolute Criteria

According to Church Growth Theory, right "proportioning of effort" in Christian mission "must be decided according to biblical principles in the light of God's revealed will" (McGavran 1970:32). But based on the premise that "a chief and irreplaceable purpose of mission is church growth", are Church Growth Theory hermeneutics truly biblical? If the "church" of McGavran's Church Growth Theory is to be seen as a sociological entity then Church Growth Theory must be subjected to strict sociological and anthropological scrutiny. But since "McGavran wants us to see the Church as *Creatio Dei*" we ought to evaluate his Church Growth Theory from a theological base. Such a theological evaluation must not from the outset jump into the thought framework of the enterprise it is trying to critique. It must begin "from above".

2. Relative Criteria

Clearly the idea of a growing church is implicit in the Gospels, but is church growth the only valid goal of mission? The Bible speaks in principle not of church growth but of Kingdom growth. Church Growth is not an instrument but a sign of mission, a necessary part of kingdom growth essential to her nature as the people of God universally.

But, is true growth to be measured in numerical terms? In Paul's "body" analogy the call to extensive growth is neither more nor less valid than the call to intensive growth, says van Engen, whose thesis is that the essential missionary "mark" of the "true church" is "yearning" rather than achievement of numerical growth (Van Engen 1981:452). Costas points out that the "numerical and organic growth in themselves do not necessarily mean that a church is indeed growing" (Costas 1982:52). The church's mission "must be evaluated not on its present institutional success but on the basis of the future of God's kingdom". To miss this point places the Church Growth Movement in danger of a "numerolatory" (Padilla 1971:104-105) patterned on the present technological society.

197

By comparison we must evaluate the assumption of Church Growth Theory that valid evangelism is only that which results in conversion.

3. Historical

Church Growth Theory must also be evaluated according to its historical contribution to mission. How well has it assisted in bringing the measurable results on which it hinges? Is it adaptable to changes in world conditions or to new insights and challenges in missionary theology?

IV. Recognized Strengths of Church Growth Theory

1. Challenge to Missionary Enterprise

Few of even its most vehement critics would deny that Church Growth Theory has contributed positively to missionary endeavour if in no other than its very effective demolition job on the traditional "mission station" approach which was a remnant of colonialism. It has called to account the pessimism of bygone days by its intentional laying aside of defeatism.

To evangelical thought in particular, Church Growth Theory has brought a new sense of direction in its passion for the redemption of souls, a reminder that the origins of mission are to be found in God. In a world beset by the phenomenon of population explosion it has brought a new sense of urgency to the missionary task.

2. Insight into Conversion

Church Growth Theory's highlighting of the social or community nature of decisions for conversion has been of incisive value particularly to the Western missionary. Church Growth Theory has also rightly recognized the value of church growth as itself a witness to the world. Missionary realism especially in modes of communication has been sought, and the call to missionary research especially in anthropology has been a valuable contribution.

3. Biblical and Social Correctives

Church Growth Theory's high view of the church has more

than a corrective value to foregoing missionary theologies which failed to promote growth of strong churches as the best preparation for changing times. And while rapid self-government and self-discipline were part of the much earlier strategy proposals of Ronald Allen, Church Growth Theory has been particularly influential in advancing these and other aspects of indigenisation.

V. Problems in Theoretical Formulations

There are however some problems at the very core of Church Growth Theory which must be considered.

1. A Shallow Hermeneutic

The hermeneutical foundation to Church Growth Theory is in McGavran's interpretation of Matt.28:18-20. Three problems in this are:

a) The isolation of three verses of scripture as a hermeneutical key.

b) The equation of "ethne" with "people groups" to interpret "panta ta ethne" as "people group by people group".

c) The adoption of "discipling" and "perfection" as separate phases in fulfilment of the commission.

2. The Theological Locus of Church Growth Theory

While Church Growth Theory has addressed quite effectively the need for new strategies in mission it has lagged behind very much in development of theological foundations. In particular for a movement with so high a view of the church there has been a dearth of ecclesiology in Church Growth Movement literature. Van Engen's contributions since 1981 are beginning to bridge this gap but a theology of conversion is also needed.

Bewildering to the outsider, Church Growth Theory terminology is often a hindrance; it clarifies only by limiting objectives. Van Engen warns that assuming the Church to be the only instrument of the Kingdom of God may lead to the same dangerous exclusivism that beset the Israel of the Old Testament (Van Engen 1981:399-400). Wagner, representing the standpoint of the more recent Church Growth Movement standpoint concedes at least in theory that Kingdom growth rather than Church Growth must be the ultimate task (Wagner 1981:59). But a sense of mystery in mission is needed to balance Church Growth Theory's fierce pragmatism; there is a self contradiction in the stress on spiritual power when the church is responsible for results.

Much Church Growth writing has concentrated on the phenomenon of growing congregations, first of all of 'large' churches, and now of 'mega' churches. Church Growth Theory's leaning toward a "might is right" mentality is unbiblical because it does not take seriously enough the eschatological tension of the church as the "little flock".

3. Truncated Concept of Mission

Church Growth Theory begins with a narrow (McGavran 1970:34) and somewhat polemical definition of mission which excludes "Service" and tends to ignore "Aid". Social action according to Church Growth Theory assumptions is good, but is the work of the church rather than mission. The assumption that "conversion" will of itself result in social improvement is unconvincing. But propositional rather than contextualised communication is an overriding assumption of Church Growth Theory.

This approach of seeing "diaconia" as an adjunct to the Gospel has been heavily criticised. "To aim at church growth is meaningless unless we are aiming in fact at Kingdom growth". As noted by Costas, "mission is fulfilled through and by the church, not through and by church growth". His reflections on the Chilean church find numerical growth concurring with escape from incarnational mission (Costas 1982:53-54). Church Growth as an end in itself edifies man rather than God. This results in a hazy view of the world into which the church is called as God's servant.

4. Developments in Church Growth Movement Position

Wagner has since begun to modify the former position saying that social ministry in accord with Kingdom values is not only as essential vocation for Christians and Christian Churches but also legitimate area of mission (Wagner 1981:94).

But whereas Wagner offers assent to Padilla's term "wholistic growth" his descriptions still indicate little integration of the "evangelistic" and "service" areas of mission; evangelism (still in a narrow sense) must have priority and the winning of multitudes remains the starting point in his Church Growth Theory (Wagner 1981:97). A closer attempt from Church Growth quarters is Yanamori's "contextual symbiosis" (cf. Wagner 1981:82,111).

5. Anthropological-Functional Syndrome

Van Engen has noted a danger in the logic of Church Growth Theory; if consequence rather than intention is made a mark of the church, struggling churches will no longer be seen as equal with "true" (growing) churches (Van Engen 1981:476-478). And if potential for growth is culturally determined, growth measurements become a thermometer of the world rather than of the church.

A bias in the language of Church Growth Theory toward the activity of North American and European rather than the so-called Third World missionary agencies spites the evidence that the great People Movements have come via indigenous lay people. The Church Growth Theory manual "Understanding Church Growth" fails really to conceive of mission in the reverse direction; nor does Church Growth Theory come to terms with the closing off of much of the world to declared missionaries.

VI. Controversial Issue: The Homogeneous Unit Principle

Although the Church Growth Movement has done a service in highlighting the importance of the Homogeneous Unit, this more than any other aspect of Church Growth Theory has come under fire.

1. Biblical View

Possibly the most effective challenge to the biblical basis for the Homogeneous Unit Principle has come from Rene Padilla (Padilla 1982). Padilla argues the essentiality of expressing church unity across cultural barriers. Such unity is exemplified in the ministry of Jesus as well as the churches of Jerusalem, Antioch,

Corinth, Rome and Paul's Gentile mission strategy, are all examples of this. McGavran's assumption that Jewish and Gentile church growth took place along separate homogeneous lines is proven invalid. Rather, the impact of Christian brotherhood across racial and cultural barriers had enormous appeal to the observing world; the Homogeneous Unit Principle is at best a posteriori biblical.

Norris' study in New Testament sociology puts the onus on the Church Growth Movement to prove the homogeneity of New Testament churches against the evidence of specialists (Norris 1983:272). The "breaking of barriers is the gospel... not just a means" (Yoder 1973:60). Failure at this point is failure to demonstrate the fullness of Christianity. To see beyond itself (as did the early Gentile mission) is evidence that a people movement is impelled by the Gospel.

2. Hermeneutics

Bosch's study of Matthew 28:16-20 shows that rather than indicating ethnic homogeneity "panta ta ethne" is intended to convey the idea of reaching far beyond the confines that existed up to that time. The People Movements, which are vital in the spread of the church in its first few centuries were also highly conscious of catholicity. Their unity was more than platonic.

Although Wagner has acknowledged this interpretation the question of the legitimacy of McGavran's hermeneutic is cautiously avoided.

3. Sociological Critique

A recent contribution to the study of Church Growth Theory is a sociological critique by Wayne McClintock (1988) who finds McGavran's definition of a People Movement hopelessly elastic and vague. The church planter is thus forced to establish his own criteria to delineate the social boundary of an Homogeneous Unit.

In McGavran's "authoritative text" a dearth of sociological and anthropological works are represented. His Homogeneous Unit concept follows many assumptions of the structural-functional school of anthropology of which "a certain vagueness about the

202

concept of boundaries around social systems" is typical. A tendency of this school is "to regard village communities as isolated units" (McClintock 1988:11). A further assumption McGavran shares is a static view of history through which past circumstances are seen as normative. The patterns which follow in the sociology of the Church Growth Theory are:

a) Neglect of the wider social and economic contexts in which Homogeneous Units exist.

b) Lack of concern with the processes of social change.

c) Simplistic and confused analysis of class structure.

d) A lack of recognition of religious and economic organisation as important elements of the social structure.

e) A view of social boundaries as rigid barriers, whereas in certain situations of ecological interdependence social interaction between ethnic groups may be highly developed.

VII. Responses to Criticism

Wagner's affirmation of heterogeneity as the ideal is to be welcomed, especially with his appeal that racially bound churches take positive steps to break down the barriers. His model of primary-homogeneous and secondary-heterogeneous relationships (Wagner 1981:112-114,172) is an attempt to come to terms with this heterogeneous ideal. But Church Growth Theory in theory and practice needs to be thoroughly reformulated if such an attempt is to be credible.

1. "Discipling Rather than Perfecting"

McGavran's use of the term "discipling" was extremely narrow. Because the discipling of a people takes place only on new ground, the conversion of each new generation is not "discipling". This distinction is misleading when read back into scripture. McGavran later refined his terminology to recognise more of a continuum between "discipling" and "perfecting". However, they still do not do justice to the nuances in Matthew 28:19. Examination of his use of related words shows that although having in mind discipling into church membership "Matthew is clearly not thinking of first-level decisions only to be followed at a later stage by a second-level decision" (Bosch 1983:231,233).

Jim Pleuddeman in biblical reflections on his experience with Church Growth Theory notes that the "first century churches seldom went on to maturity in Christ without deep spiritual struggle". "Growth is an inner process and cannot be forced... We have much to learn about fostering spiritual growth without forcing it" (Pleuddeman 1987:35).

2. Prioritising

A biblical basis for "win the winnable" is found in Church Growth thought only by analogy, and that, with considerable exegesis. Although the winnable and the poor often coincide a priority based on receptivity also spites the biblical concern for the realities of the life of the poor. Priority toward the receptive should also be held lightly against the priority of guidance by the Holy Spirit so clear in Acts (eg. 16:6-10).

Adaptation of Church Growth Theory should be determined by contextualisation requiring the missionary to identify with the limited resources as well as the people. The strategy "win the winnable" doesn't work, says Goldsmith, first because it is relative and secondly because it ignores God's guidance. In his study of the Karo Homogeneous Unit, early evangelism was fruitless yet a dramatic movement followed later (Goldsmith 1983:39).

VIII. Conclusion

Church Growth Theory has been found useful as a tool in mission strategy but as with any tool the results will depend not only on its inherent value but also on continual sharpening and improvement as well as discerning use. The dangers are that the tool be used indiscriminately or that the tool rather than the user determines the work done. The danger with Church Growth Theory is that sociological rather than biblical criteria come to define conversion, and statistics to define the goals of mission.

If Church Growth Theory is going to be biblically wholistic it must promote qualities of spirituality, incarnation and faithfulness, measured in organic, mental and diaconal as well as numerical growth.

So although Church Growth Theory has channelled valuable contributions to the science of missions it is doubtful whether it can be upheld as the basis of a biblically coherent strategy without radical reformation. It has functioned positively as a rallying point for evangelical missiologists at a time of uncertainty but those who rallied to this point would do well to look beyond it in faithfulness to Scripture and its Lord.

References

Bosch, David J. (1983) "The Structure of Mission: an Exposition of Matthew 28:16-20" in W.R. Shenk (ed.), *Exploring Church Growth*, Grand Rapids: Eerdmans, pp.231, 233.

Costas, Orlando E. (1982) *Christ Outside the Gate.* New York: Orbis, p.52.

Goldsmith, Martin F. (1983) "The Karo Batak" in W.R. Shenk (ed.), *Exploring Church Growth*, Grand Rapids: Eerdmans, p.38.

McGavran, Donald Anderson (1970) *Understanding Church Growth,* Grand Rapids: Eerdmans, p.32.

McGavran, Donald Anderson (1955) *The Bridges of God,* World Dominion Press.

McClintock, Wayne (1988) "Sociological Critique of the Homogeneous Unit Principle" in *International Review of Missions* Vol.77 No.305, pp.11,112-115.

Norris, F.W. (1983) "Strategy for Mission in the New Testament" in W.R. Shenk (ed.), *Exploring Church Growth*, Grand Rapids: Eerdmans, p.272.

Padilla, Rene C. (1982) "The Unity of the Church and the Homogeneous Unit Principle" in *International Bulletin of Missionary Research,* Vol.6 No.1.

Padilla, Rene C. (1971) "A Step Climb Ahead for Theology in Latin America" in *Evangelical Missions Quarterly*, Vol.7 No.2.

Pickett, J. Waskom (1933) *Christian Mass Movements in India,* Lucknow: Lucknow Publishing House.

Pleuddeman, James E. (1987) "Needed, An Enlarged View of Church Growth" in *Evangelical Missions Quarterly,* Vol.23 No.1, p.35.

Wagner, C.P. (1980) "Recent Developments in Church Growth Understandings", in *Review and Expositor,* Vol.77 No.4 p.43.

Wagner, C.P. (1981) *Church Growth and the Whole Gospel,* San Francisco: Harper & Row.

Yoder, J.H. (1973) "Church Growth Issues in Theological Perspective" in W.R. Shenk (ed.), *The Challenge of Church Growth*, Scottsdale: Herald, p.60.

CHAPTER 12

Group Discussions

I. Spirituality of Struggle

Members: John Poovatholil, Surya Prakash, Mary Lobo, Joseph Valiamangalam

India has a great spiritual heritage and we have much to learn from the wisdom of the people. Among people who are sick, marginalised and are struggling for survival, for a fuller life, for food and shelter, and those who are exploited in the name of caste, creed and religious beliefs, we find that they are full of hope and trust in God. And we feel solidarity with them and are touched by their struggles for survival. We are walking with all kinds of oppressed people but often feel helpless not knowing what to do. We come across many committed people of other religious faiths and ideologies who have dedicated their life for the cause of the poor. Their life and works inspire us and help us get out of our narrow-mindedness, ghetto mentality and rigid structures.

The deep religious faith and God-experience of the marginalised is expressed through prayers, fasting, festivals, pilgrimages and solidarity among themselves; these help them to go on in spite of certain negative elements in popular religiosity.

The life situation of the poor and the powerless constantly challenges us to live our commitment to the spirituality of Incarnation and especially the *kenosis* of Christ.

1. Shakti and Missionary Spirituality

God's creative power has been experienced by the people of India from ancient times as *Shakti*. This power of God invites us to participate in it to liberate us from all evil and be united with

Him/Her. The powerless need to be empowered and we see the divine manifestation of empowerment through the expression of *Shakti* in the movement of dalit women and tribals. We need a spirituality of empowerment in the light of the gospel values of equality, dignity and empowerment practised by the first Christians as narrated in the Acts of the Apostles.

We have to draw many good elements from peoples' religion or movements, for example, devotion to *devi*, their vision of whole creation as something holy, and the solidarity and community sense that support them in their struggles. Hence we have to stress communitarian spirituality more than the individualistic.

2. Worship As Other Centredness

Even our worship must put us in touch with the outward realities of life. The Spirit of God is already at work in all people. Hence worship is a meeting of all people as community of brothers and sisters.

3. Emerging Forms of Indian Missionary Spirituality

Today in the various Churches of India we come across various spiritual movements containing emerging forms of missionary spirituality. Some of these forms are: the ashram movement, the charismatic movement, the movements for social transformation, and the movements based on ecological concern. All these movements help the Church to live out its mission in various contexts, such as religious pluralism, need for renewal of faith, social injustice and the need to preserve harmony in nature. We see also more people of different religious backgrounds come together on a common platform for the same common causes, goals and values. This will help us to come together and to build a new human community based on the values of the Kingdom of God.

II. Mission and Kingdom: Symbols and Presence of Kingdom Communities, Mission and Unity, Church and Kingdom.

Members: James Chacko, Joseph Mattam, Sebastian Kim, F. Hrangkhuma, Anto Karokaran

1. Preamble

Even after 50 years of independence the majority of our people live in inhuman conditions due to religious, social and economic exploitation, casteism, injustice and communalism.

2. Presence of Kingdom Communities

In this context, recognising God at work in the people's life and struggles and responding to his desire for the wholeness of humans in society, living with dignity as brothers and sisters and sharing the earth, and inspired by the life, mission and values of Jesus and moved by his Spirit we work to form communities where human beings are respected, can live in dignity, where equality and justice reign, where people join in the struggles for the wholeness of people and for a decent human living; where people are enabled to grow in faith, hope and love for fellow humans; where people are freed from fears of every kind, hatred, fear of spirits, fatalism, communal division and other forms of enslavement. In these communities people join in activities for the betterment of all, celebrate together their success, share the pain and suffering, join in national festivals and celebrations; join also in religious celebrations of others, whenever and to the extent possible. This is the process which goes on deepening and extending towards greater fullness.

3. Mission and Unity of Believers and Liberation

In this process all Christians of the locality come together, irrespective of their denominations and are committed to the cause of God's reign. They respect each others' differences. They also join followers of other religions for the cause of liberation. Ecumenism will take new forms when Christians come together and work for God's cause, even when doctrinal differences persist and are respected. We encourage Christians to seek deeper unity in worship and service and appreciate each others' religious experiences.

We have to be on the alert that there are groups which may not share this vision and may cause division. Mission is not seen primarily as territorial expansion but as transformation of value systems opposed to the concerns of the kingdom and areas of human life with their diversities, problems and challenges.

4. Growth of Christian Communities as Leaven and Salt

While we oppose any form of cohesion and fraud in getting new members, we desire Jesus Christ to be known and accepted by more and more people. We emphasize the deepening of Christian life among Christians who live in love and support each other and reach out to all irrespective of religious affiliation. We want the growth of the community of disciples of Jesus Christ who accept him and the values of the Kingdom. We are opposed to the growth of this community at the expense of the cultures and identity of various groups of people of our land. While we are immersed in the lives of the people as salt and leaven, we also recognize our responsibility to critique whatever is opposed to human growth and values of the Kingdom and thus create a counter culture which opposes all types of discrimination. The churches need to keep renewing themselves, their structures, attitudes and theology to manifest more and more the values of the Kingdom in their own life and thus be the light, leaven and salt that Jesus wanted them to be.

III. A Missionary Christology

Members: Mar Osthathios, Joseph Patmury, Jacob Kavunkal, Jesuino Almeida, Antony Kalliath

1. The Context and Perspective

The context of a missionary christology is indeed the religio-cultural pluralism and the socio-economic challenges of our society. Understanding Christ and the revelation realised in the Christ event in correlation with world religions is the perspective of a missionary christology.

2. Methodology

Methodology is vital while envisaging a missionary christology. In the theological literature we can find different traditional patterns of presenting Christ, namely, exclusivism, parallelism and inclusivism. These patterns have become obsolete in the face of today's pluralism. It is felt that Jesus' own methodology is the most conducive and appropriate while thinking about a missionary christology in a context of pluralism.

We can infer twin profiles in the proclamation of the Good News by Jesus, namely, the common Fatherhood/Motherhood and the centrality of the Kingdom of God. Needless to say, since these two dimensions embody innately trans-religious and trans-cultural nuances, the Good News became spontaneously fascinating and welcoming to everybody, the Jews, the Greeks, the Gentiles and the poor, i.e., to all classes of society. To phrase it in the present idiom, Jesus' Good News was interreligious to the core. The methodology of the missionary christology should not fail to focus on these twin emphases, especially the centrality of the reign of God.

3. Jesus' Relatedness to Reality

While envisioning a missionary christology, first and foremost the radical relatedness of Jesus to humanity and its existential concerns should be the prime focus. Jesus' relatedness is fundamentally unfolded in his kingdom ministry of *koinonia* and *diakonia*. It has been a christology of solidarity and fellowship with the marginalized and victimised.

This ministry of Jesus' solidarity with human concerns and suffering acquires credibility in the ministry of his *kenosis* which is a radical eucharistic sharing (took + blessed + broke + gave) as well.

Moreover, missionary christology has a Trinitarian dimension. It is through the ministry of *kenosis*, i.e., self-emptying for sharing that the Trinitarian life of communion becomes operative in the realization of the kingdom of God. Hence missionary christology is a christology of kingdom ministry which proclaims Jesus' relatedness to the Reality in the Trinitarian mystery.

4. Role of the Holy Spirit

A missionary christology is fundamentally a pneumatic christology. That is to say, our Christian witness in the christic relatedness to Reality can be realised in a pneumatic realm.

To elaborate, in the mystery of the Christ event we can find twin pneumatic phases: the first, *kenosis* i.e., the Word becoming incarnate in human flesh; the second, the Word transcends 'human flesh' — Jewish particularity, i.e., the mystery of Resurrection. In both these phases the Spirit is the prime agent.

It is particularly through the second phase of transcending the Jewish specificity that Jesus of Nazareth became the Christ, the cosmic principle. Thus the Word became vibrant and dynamic in the relatedness of Reality. The Word as the dynamic principle of the innate relatedness of Reality is the mystery of the Word's trans-historical and trans-cultural presence. This is our interreligious faith which should motivate us to search Christ in an interreligious realm. Then, the second phase of the Christ event demands us that we Christians admit the mystery of the risen Christ not as a private possession of Christianity. As the resurrected one, the Word is present and operative in the whole of Reality.

A missionary christology therefore inspires us to participate in the Word's cosmic presence, beyond the Jewishness of the Incarnate word, in the genius of world religions and cultures. This universal presence of the Word Incarnate is the pneumatic dimension of the missionary christology.

5. Missionary Christology and the Imperative of Dialogue

Since the risen Jesus has transcended the historical specificity and became a cosmic principle in the interrelatedness of Reality, the mystery of Jesus is revealed in a trans-religious spectrum. It implies that Christianity can deepen its comprehension of Jesus' mystery in a dialogical relationship with the totality of Reality which includes world religions, human history, struggles of liberation and human scientific endeavour.

A missionary christology therefore entails a culture of partnership and fellowship with all kinds of human pursuits of Truth, both religious and secular for the fuller glow and glory of the Christ event.

Fundamentally it is our rootedness in and faithfulness to Christ that impels us to envisage a missionary christology. It is only in this spectrum of dialogical co-existence and of common pilgrimage of religions that a Christian can experience and realize the mystery of Christ in its fullness and depth.

Contributors and Participants

Fr Anto Karokaran, CMI
Ishvani Kendra
P.O. Box 3003
Pune 411 014

Fr Joseph Puthenpurackal, SDB
Sacred Heart Theological College,
Mawlai, Shillong
Meghalya 793 008

Sr Mary Lobo, MCJ
Nari Jagran Manch
Pachatti, Bodh Gaya
Gaya Dt., Bihar 824 231

Dr Atul Aghamkar
Pune Tyrannus Hall
27, Gidney Park
Pune 411 037

Dr Joseph Patmury
United Theological College
63 Miller's Road
Bangalore 560 046

Fr Julian Saldanha, SJ
St. Pius College
Goregaon East
Mumbai 400 063

Rev Sebastian Kim
Union Biblical Seminary
Post Box 1425, Bibvewadi,
Pune 411 037

Fr Joseph Valiamangalam, SJ
Premal Jyoti
P.B. 4002, Ahmedabad 380 009

Fr G. Lazar, SVD
Divine Word Seminary
Pune 411 014

Fr Antony Kalliath
Dharmaram College
Dharmaram College P.O.
Bangalore 560 029

Fr Jacob Kavunkal, SVD
Institute of Indian Culture
Mahakali Rd, Andheri (E)
Mumbai 400 093

Dr F. Hrangkhuma
Theology Department
Serampore College
Serampore 712 201, W.B.

Fr Joseph Mattam, SJ
Premal Jyoti
P.B. 4002
Ahmedabad 380 009

Fr Joy Thomas, SVD
Ishvani Kendra
Post Box 3003
Pune 411 014

Dr. Surya Prakash
United Theological College
63 Miller's Road
Bangalore 560 046

Met. G. Mar Osthathios
St Paul's Mission,
Training Centre
P.O. Mavelikara
Kerala 690 103

Fr Jesuino Almeida, SFX
Mata Mariam
Jan Seva Vidyalaya
P.Box 6, Narnaul
Haryana 123 001

Rev James Chacko
C.O.T.R. Theological Seminary
Dora Thota, Post Box 3
Bhimili P.O. Vizag 531 163, A.P.

Fr John Poovatholil, CMI
Provincial House
Bellampalli P.O.,
Adilabad Dt., A.P. 504 251